Sprint to the Finish

Sprint to the Finish

Penny and David Eisenstein

iUniverse, Inc.
New York Lincoln Shanghai

Sprint to the Finish

iUniverse books may be ordered through booksellers or by contacting:

iUniverse
2021 Pine Lake Road, Suite 100
Lincoln, NE 68512
www.iuniverse.com
1-800-Authors (1-800-288-4677)

ISBN: 0-595-33213-7 (pbk)
ISBN: 0-595-66774-0 (cloth)

Printed in the United States of America

Contents

.

1

Sprinting to that Finish Line

✦

(Practical actions toward amassing assets so even late starters can retire!)

Retirement! For many, the idea was so far into the future that it was given little thought and subsequently little planning was done to prepare for it. But here it comes, like a train rolling down a mountain track, ready or not!

No need to panic as there are ways to accomplish what needs to be done to retire with peace of mind. If we, as an estate attorney and a financial planner, have learned anything in our respective practices of helping people achieve their financial goals, it is that people have a multitude of opportunities to make retirement a wonderful experience. Man's resourcefulness is astounding and we look forward to sharing ideas and knowledge with you.

It is never too late to begin to prepare for that retirement time and this book will offer a myriad of different actions to get you there, some conventional and some creative. We also cite case studies, as knowing what others with similar goals have accomplished helps us to feel encouraged and motivated.

This is not the usual wealth planning "how to" book. While we discuss the mechanics of wealth accumulation and investing, just as importantly we include a lot of out of the box thinking to generate practical tips to help you sprint to the finish line.

2

Getting Started!

Many people have a good idea of how they want to spend their retirement. Do you intend to sip margaritas on a Florida beach? Are you intending to travel to far-off lands to experience different cultures and landscapes? Is staying close to home and hearth with family and friends what appeals to you? Do you want the challenges of new skills, such as taking up golf or scuba diving or bass fishing? Will you settle in your current home or relocate? Is hitting the road in a motor home a lifestyle that excites you? Will you continue to work part-time?

Research has shown that we Americans are eternal optimists when it comes to our retirement. Research further shows that only less than half of us have calculated how much money we will need to have saved by the time we retire in order to have that lifestyle we desire. In fact, people seem to spend more time planning for holidays and vacations than retirement.

Most of us didn't learn about retirement planning from our parents because it wasn't much of an issue for past generations. However we now have medical knowledge and technology to help us live longer and more actively, but that creates a need for more funds in our retirement pot.

How Much Do I Need?

One fallacy of retirement planning is that people expect to spend less than they did while they were working. Study after study shows that at least in the early years of retirement, people tend to spend the same and sometimes more. While we may shop less for clothes for the office and the gasoline to get there, new retirees are apt to expend more dollars on travel and new hobbies. People nearing retirement also like to buy a new car if they can pay cash for it. For some individuals, dealing with increased medical costs as we age becomes an added expenditure.

Maintaining a quality of life in retirement will mean different things to different people.

The American Association of Retired People (AARP) has recently released a study that looks at key indicators of quality of life for people 50 and older. The study also measures changes to these variables over the past 10 years (1992-2002). Let's see what the researchers found.

Median family income has increased over the years of the study by almost 12%, going from $32,000 in 1992 to $35,800 in 2002. But the study segregated income into two groups: ages 50 to 64 and 65 and older. Not surprising, the former group are mostly still working and that group's income was more than twice that of the older group.

More than half of the population age 62 or older relies on Social Security for more than 50% of their income and nearly half the workforce age 50 and older has no pension plan. These statistics are not surprising as pension plans are rarely offered by employers anymore. Pensions are costly to the employers and have been replaced in most cases by a company 401-k plan. If you do have a pension plan due you in retirement, be glad as they are worth their weight in gold! Most pensions have life time benefits for the employee, and sometimes will provide a lessened benefit for the spouse during their lifetime. You will want to know exactly what benefits are available for you and your spouse as the plans can differ dramatically.

A major factor affecting the quality of life in retirement is how healthy you are. About 50% of the respondents over age 50 said they felt "very good" or "excellent". Of the 65 and older group, 38% gave those same responses.

Internet surfing will allow you to keep up with the grandchildren and the world at large. Between 1998 and 2002, the percentage of people over 50 who have Internet access at home sprang from 15% to 47%.

Although the percentage of older Americans living alone has increased over the past decades, more than two thirds were very satisfied with their amount of family contact.

Nearly one third surveyed suffered financial losses in 2003. Nine percent of those already retired contemplated going back to work. Those not already retired plan to retire later than those already retired.

You don't want to be one of those aimlessly drifting into retirement, or worse, having to re-enter the workforce reluctantly after you retire.

Therefore:

Focus on the lifestyle you want for your retirement as this will give you a goal to work towards. If you don't set that rudder, your boat could just go in circles. Take some time to ponder about what you truly enjoy. Let yourself dream of things you wish to accomplish or experience. Visualize your lifestyle in retirement. If you are married, include your spouse in these thoughts.

Let's take the example of Lori and John, aged 61 and 63 respectively. They have worked long and hard, but haven't saved much of a nest egg. Their goals are to remain in the western U.S. to be somewhat close to their families in the Los Angeles area; to be able to maintain a low key retirement lifestyle as they are "homebodies"; and reside in an area that doesn't have weather issues.

Since they do not have much in the way of savings, they decided that once they retired, they would sell their current home in Southern California and use the equity to buy a smaller, lest costly residence. They are looking into the Arizona and Oregon markets for such alternatives. With those general parameters in mind, they next need to determine at what age retirement becomes feasible for them.

Let's travel with them as they consider various options.

3

Take Action Now!

Lori and John are working their way toward the big picture, but every day retirement gets closer and there are things that can be done immediately to bring them (and you!) closer to the retirement of your choosing.

It's time to take action now!

Get rid of your boats, airplanes, motorcycles, recreational vehicles, mountain cabin, and country club memberships unless they play a very important part in your current lifestyle. For example, you can rent a sail boat three or four times a year for less than it costs to own one. Often items like motorcycles, off road vehicles, and classic cars sit in a garage collecting dust after the initial thrill of ownership has passed. Sell them and put the cash in investments that make your money work for you. An additional benefit is that you can eliminate maintenance costs such as insurance and storage rental.

While we are strong proponents of owning investment real estate, there is a difference between good and bad properties. Good property means the cash flow is sufficient to cover your expenses and the property is appreciating in value. Bad property is that condo you bought for a second home that has neither of the aforementioned qualities. Bad property is the cabin at the lake or in the mountains that you bought in a partnership that is giving you problems and no money! Bad property is that lot you bought to someday retire on but you no longer desire to retire there. Sell them. Get rid of the anxiety of dealing with them. It is amazing how apathy, or of having to admit to oneself that an error in judgment was made, will keep people from cutting their losses and moving on. You will read it several times in this book—less mess makes for less stress. One of the key ingredients for a peaceful life is keeping things simple!

Gift Giving Problems

Use common sense with gift giving. David and I both have seen clients who love to shower their family with gifts but when that gift giving interferes with sound financial planning, it can be problematic. I remember one story a client told us regarding this issue. When they were in their mid 50s, the husband received sizable bonuses for several years in a row. For the holidays those years they gave their adult children and their spouses and grandchildren some really terrific gifts. The kids and grandchildren were excited and delighted and grateful. In future years the bonuses declined but having set the expectation of the spectacular gifts, they were embarrassed to lower the gift giving amounts. Eventually they had to be practical but it was a painful experience for them.

It is relatively easy to tell your young child "no." Helping out your adult children when they run into life's challenges is a more difficult situation. Much as we would like to, we can't shield our children from the ups and downs in life. And there is plenty of research that indicates trying to save them from all difficulties actually takes away their opportunity to be a problem solver and the subsequent good feeling accomplishment brings. Particularly if your retirement savings are on the slim side, your kids may be better served by your keeping that investment working for you now so you don't have to go TO THEM for help in your later years.

Use common sense when gifting to spouses, yes spouses! A couple who recently came to our office had run up inordinate amounts in credit card charges, which they couldn't afford. Many of the purchases were unreasonable for a couple closing in on retirement with limited funds—an $8,500 diamond ring for an anniversary for her, lavish costs for a large birthday celebration for him. Presenting your spouse with grand gifts is not a substitute for love and consideration; more gifts do not mean more love. David and I are not psychologists (but after years of working with families one tends to learn some practical intuitions) and this kind of spending, rather than strengthening a relationship, will eventually add to marital discord.

Spenders and Savers

Sometimes a couple will have money problems in that one of them loves to "buy" and the other watches every penny. While this may cause some intense discussions between them, they may be fortunate in that the spending pendulum probably doesn't swing too far in either direction if they can peaceably compromise.

The couples more at risk are those who both love to spend with abandon. Without a check and balance, trouble will not be far off. One client, Carol, told us after a recent divorce that the thing she and her ex-husband did best together was to spend money, a truly sad commentary. We can't buy respect/love/fun/comfort/peace.

We are all raised differently so it stands to reason we will not necessarily have the same attitudes on how to manage money. Retirement does not change this—in fact, since there are no longer opportunities to have salary increases or bonuses to make up for bad judgment spending, these money issues can become more emotionally distressing. If you fall into this category we urge you to tackle the problem head on and make yourselves work through it before retirement time arrives.

If you still have children at home, sometimes there is a conflict of where to put savings. You want to start a college fund but you know you need to fund your own IRAs or 401-ks. If you can do both, that is wonderful but if that is not practical, fill your retirement plans first and don't feel guilty. You cannot get a school grant, or student loan, for your retirement.

Vacation Time Shares

If you don't own one, we generally don't recommend you go buy one. Your "share" does not accrue depreciation tax benefits like other investment real estate, your share generally will not appreciate in value, and if you need to sell it quickly (if a couple is divorcing, or has had a financial set back or there has been a death of a spouse, the time share is usually the first thing to go) you might only get a fraction of what you paid for it. If you are determined to buy a time share, check out the companies that do the resales as you can save greatly on the prices.

For some, however, time shares can work well. If you have children who vacation with you, most time share facilities are minimum one bedroom with a pull out couch in the living room and a kitchen. That can be more economical than renting two hotel rooms and eating every meal in a restaurant. If you are unable to use your week, you normally can have the facility rent out your space and pay you something, albeit not much, for it. A better cash situation for you might be to rent it out to a friend or family yourself, but check first as some places prohibit that practice. Time shares only earn their keep if you make use of your week; don't put off making reservations and lose your ability to use your space for the year. If you are avid travelers, you can exchange your week at your resort for a week at a resort in another location. Two years ago we personally did an exchange for a place in Italy and saved considerably over what a hotel for seven nights would have cost. And again, having the cooking capability contributed to that savings. If you wish to research the exchange options, a company called RCI is well known for worldwide access to resorts. See RCI.com.

Painless Prosperity!

Gift yourself! This next process is relatively painless but so very beneficial. When you receive money gifts, salary increases or bonuses, tax returns, inheritances, reimbursement for business expenses, and purchase rebates, quickly put them in savings. You were surviving before you got them so pretend you don't have them to spend. It will amaze you the way that savings account will grow.

People Magazine wrote "A latte spurned is a fortune earned." Save some of that money that is so easily dribbled away without giving it much thought. Have a latte once a week instead of every day and save the difference. It will add up and you will be pleased.

When you pay off a car loan or a credit card, put that money into savings also. You were living without it before and you can do it now.

Take advantage of coupons and purchase rebates. A majority of people do not use purchase rebates yet they can return a hefty amount, particularly if you are buying appliances or electronics. If your newspaper doesn't have enough coupons, try Coolsavings.com for added savings.

And when buying those appliances you may want to pass on the maintenance contracts that the sales people will try to sell you. Reputable products will automatically carry a year's warranty and you can further protect yourself by using a credit card to make the purchase. If you have a problem you normally can contest the purchase to your credit company if done within 60 days of the sale. Maintenance contracts are extremely lucrative for manufacturers so that should tell you what you need to know about that story.

Spring Cleaning!

Clean out your closets! How can that be an advantage to you? First pack up the clothes and sundry items you are discarding in boxes or plastic bags and call a local charity to pick them up. The charity will give you a letter as proof of the contribution which you can use on your next income tax return for a charitable deduction tax savings. Everyone wins. There are some limitations but normally it is pretty simple. Another benefit is that cluttered houses nurture cluttered minds—less mess, less stress!

Use a credit card that accumulates Frequent Flier Miles if you enjoy traveling. Several companies such as Capital One or Advantage, can offer the miles as part of the benefits of their credit cards at no additional cost. Our personal feeling is that most of the airline specific cards are more restrictive in that you can only fly that airline and it is difficult to accumulate lots of points on just one airline to meet their minimums for redemption. Plus airline companies have been known to go out of business! It pays to compare the various plans.

While on the subject of credit cards, if you are disciplined and pay off the balance each month, we definitely recommend you use one. It is a good tool to monitor your monthly spending.

Easy Savings!

Robin and Bob, good friends of ours who live in Newport Beach, gave us a tip that we personally instigated in our own lives. We are avid readers, as they are. They can afford to buy all the books they want but they go to the library for their reading material. Not only does it save money, but it also eliminates the problem of what to do with the books once you are finished with them. How many book-shelves can a house have? Another rather surprising benefit is that the library's ambience offers a quiet, peaceful respite from the world. It's a pleasure to be there.

Try to limit your restaurant dining. Research after research has shown that dining out is the leading hidden expense of consumers. We do it more frequently than we think we do and we spend inordinately more than we think we do. When you need to dine out, if you can pick up the food and bring it home you may have left-overs for another meal and you also save the costs of beverages (e.g. $7.50 for a glass of wine) and tipping.

Do you like to go to the movies? With movie tickets as high as $10, plus the "in the movie theatre" lure of expensive popcorn and drinks and candy, you may save a bundle by renting movies at home. Both cable and satellite have a multitude of movie packages. There also are companies that will send you DVDs in the mail at considerable savings. Contact Netflix, a company that sends the movies directly to your home for about $20 per month.

Use senior discounts! Sometimes as early as age 50 or 55 you can qualify for discounts for airfare, hotels, car rentals, movies, and restaurants just by asking. You can also join the AARP, an association that provides its members with a wealth of information about bargains and discounts. Call them at (800) 424-3410 or email at member@aarp.org.

Stay Hitched!

Unless you are married to an Atilla the Hun, or Atilly the Hunette, don't get divorced! The popular and well researched book "The Millionaire Next Door" by Drs. T. Stanley and W. Danko, states the majority of millionaires in the U.S. are in a category of "one house, one spouse".

They further report most millionaires buy used vehicles as opposed to new. We couldn't agree more! That new leather smell can be costly. We think the best deal is a car with under 20,000 miles on the odometer—it will carry the same new car warranty without the new car sticker price. If you have access to the internet, it is simple to research local dealers to find a vehicle having your parameters for sale.

Pay cash for your automobiles, especially as you get closer to retirement. Remember there are things in retirement that must be paid on a continuing basis—utilities, homeowner insurance, automobile insurance, long term care insurance, life insurance, property taxes, income taxes, food, medical expenses, gasoline, personal grooming, gifts, pet maintenance, home maintenance and so forth. Eliminating as much debt as possible will enable you to deal with the recurring costs more effectively.

We like this short story to make an important point. There are two identical families (Dad, Mom, two children) who live next door to each other in identical houses, who earn the same amount of income and who drive identical cars. Why is one family living from paycheck to paycheck and the other family has a nice fat retirement account? TIMING! Family One buys what they want when they want it; Family Two waits until they have the cash, thereby saving interest and finance charges and is often able to negotiate a better price by offering cash.

4

Dealing with Debt

Before jumping on the debt issue, let's clarify Bad Debt and Good (relatively speaking) Debt. Your home mortgage and student loans are the usual acceptable Good Debt. Auto loans and credit card balances are Bad Debt. In a perfect world, the Good Debt means you bought something with borrowed funds that will appreciate in value.

The majority of us have debt but the challenge is to figure out how much is too much. The Credit Union National Association gives a guideline for maximum comfort debt load, excluding your home, to not exceed 20% of your take home pay. Many financial planners espouse 10% being a better number.

They advise consumers to include second mortgages and home equity loans in the mix when they measure their debt load using the 20 percent rule. The reason they say this is that while a first mortgage is generally on a property that in many cases is appreciating in value, second mortgages are more likely the owner's attempt to pay off unsecured debt, like credit cards.

In our office we see people at a 5% level and others at a 25% level. Each person's tolerance for debt might be slightly different and there can be different circumstances for different people.

A person's income will have an effect too. People in an upper income level have more access to credit, but they have more ability to pay it off. "Someone with a higher salary might be in a position to take on a higher percentage of debt because there may be more discretionary income" says Rus Halsey, a manager for GreenPath Debt Solutions, a nonprofit credit counseling service. But even these people should be wary.

Several studies estimate that at least 10 percent of Americans are in serious trouble with debt, and that does not necessarily assume that the other 90 percent are managing their funds exceedingly well.

Let's look at some of the warning signs that you need to be aware of:

You don't have enough cash each month to pay all your bills. That means you are overspending. If you start to use credit for bill paying, you are in a danger zone. Ideally credit is there to help us monitor our spending, allow us to not have to carry a lot of cash, acquire frequent flier miles or credits, and extend payments for major purchases, such as an automobile, over a manageable period of time.

You are rarely able to pay off the credit card balance each month. Occasionally that will happen to all of us but if it becomes consistent, it means you are spending more than your cash flow allows. Even worse is if you are at the stage of only being able send in the minimums due each month. If you are using credit cards to pay other credit card debt it is a sure sign of serious trouble.

Have you started to buy groceries with a credit card because you don't have the cash? Are you at the limit, or close to it, on your credit cards? You may have charged yourself into a corner.

Are you running up unsecured lines of credit, such as overdraft protection? If so, you are losing that last battle line of financial assistance if a crisis hits your family.

Are you considering a consolidation loan to lessen the monthly struggle? Perhaps this will be another consolidation loan. Note that people often do a consolidation loan but if they don't change their spending habits, they will be in the same position all over again.

Have you been denied credit or asked for a co-signer in order to get new credit? If creditors don't think you have enough money to repay them they probably are right.

Are you and your spouse fighting over money issues? If couples are fighting about spending, there is a problem that needs to be addressed. Are you physically ill? Ric Edelman, author of the The Truth About Money, says "anxiety is healthy as it shows the brain is recognizing your spending patterns are in conflict with your income. The problem is for many people that indebtedness doesn't bother them".

Others may feel pain about their financial situation but aren't sure how to deal with it. So if you start getting anxious, listen to your gut feelings. It's time to stop the bleeding!

Debt can be managed!

The first principal you must grasp is that you have to spend less than you earn. You need to recognize that you cannot continue with your same spending habits and expect to pull yourself out of the dilemma you presently are faced with. There is an old saying that a person who thinks he can continue with his same actions but expects a different result is a fool. You are not a fool. You are going to attack this problem and get the results you need to move forward in your life.

Keep one credit card for emergencies but cut up ALL the others, including department store cards! Yes, it's painful but it is a major step in the right direction. Tell yourself that if you do not have the cash, you cannot afford it!

Eliminate old debt. Pay off those old credit card bills as fast as you can. Your ultimate goal is to have a zero balance every month end! When determining which cards to pay off, the most logical thing is getting rid of the cards with the highest interest charge. However, David and I feel another approach will better help some people and that is to get rid of those having the smallest balances first. There is big psychological boost in being able to cut up and throw away a credit card! It also means receiving one less bill in the mail to have to look at. If that works better for you, do it! The goal is to get rid of debt and whatever motivates you most is the way to go. Be sure to call and cancel the paid off cards as cutting them up will not get the account closed or off your credit report, even if you are no longer charging on them.

Avoid new debt. Try to make that old computer or washing machine work until you have the cash to buy the new ones. It will save you financing charges. It will make you stop and think about whether you really need the new item. It will help keep you from impulse buying. It will give you time to scout out the best prices for when you do buy it.

Spend prudently. A wise friend of mine, Beverly, who loves to shop, but in spite of that, has rules to which she adheres: She won't buy an article of clothing unless it fits and looks absolutely great! It must be "special" she says. All of us have clothes that we purchased even though we didn't really like them at the time. Keeping them in the closet won't make you like them any more in the future than you did when you originally bought them. Often Beverly will have a store "hold" the merchandise for her until the next day to give her time to reflect on its merit. That often allows her to realize she can live quite nicely without the purchase. Her second rule is don't buy things for the home unless they are necessary. Sound harsh? How many accessories and electronics and house wares do you have that are sitting in drawers, closets or the garage that you bought on a whim?

Spread out all your monthly credit card bills on the table. If any of them are reflecting an interest rate being charged of over 13%, call the company and say you would like to stay with them but you have access to lower interest cards. Ask them what they can do for you to bring down the interest rate you currently are paying. They may not react very friendly, but if you are persistent, you very well may get a lesser interest rate. It certainly is worth the call.

If you have gotten yourself into an uncomfortable financial place, don't be discouraged. We know from working with a multitude of clients that these situations can be resolved. David and I have clients that have an income of $30,000 and who manage to be debt-free, yet others with $200,000$_+$ incomes that spend $300,000 annually. It's not what you make but how much you spend that makes the difference in debt management.

Personally, I don't like budgets. The word conjures up negative thoughts like denial or sacrifice. Bottom line, you are an adult. You will know, if you put some effort forth, what you can or cannot afford. If that is hard for you to determine, go back to the basics. No cash, no buy! This bears repeating, no cash, no buy! This will get you back on the track to financial health.

Credit is important!

While we are on the subject, credit is a necessity of living the good life. In years past credit reports were pulled primarily when someone was looking for a home or car loan or a credit card. Now, your credit report will be pulled when you are applying for insurance, renting an apartment, having utilities turned on or making application for employment. Having good credit definitely extends benefits to you.

The higher your credit score, also known as FICO score, the better credit applicant you are considered to be. Surpassing a 700 to 720 score will give you borrowing power at the best rates.

Here are ways to keep your scores high:

First, check your credit score. You can order a report from myfico.com or through one of the three credit agencies:
Equifax, P.O. Box 105873, Atlanta, Georgia 30348 (800) 685-1111
Online at www.econsumer.equifax.com

Experian, P.O. Box 949, Allen, TX 75013-0949
(800) 643-3334
Online at www.experian.com

Trans Union Corporation, P.O. Box 390, Springfield, PA 19064-0390
(800) 682-7654
Online at www.transunion.com

Pay your bills on time. The longer you go without a late payment, the better your score. This is important as it represents about 35% of your score.

Don't apply for more cards. Every time you apply for credit, the lender pulls your score. Shopping for a mortgage or a car loan won't get you in trouble, but multiple card inquiries can lower your score by up to 10%.

Don't use all of your available credit. Pay your balances down. Don't cancel all your cards (unless you have a problem with debt!!!) as it reduces your available credit and can lower your score by 30%.

Don't jump around from card company to card company. If you have at least one card that is more than two years old it will help your score by as much as 15%.

Don't borrow on margin on your investment brokerage account to buy stocks! You may be reading this and wondering who in the world would do that? In the tech boom of 1999 a lot of people did and a lot of those same people are still paying off the loans. Bad idea.

5

Are You Too Young to Retire?

Our couple, Lori and John, need to consider other issues as they put their dreams and hopes in focus. And as for most people, Social Security is a factor in their retirement planning.

In a recent survey, approximately 80% of Americans either incorrectly guessed or didn't know their eligibility age for full Social Security retirement benefits.

Legislation passed in 1983 makes those born after 1960 not eligible to receive full Social Security benefits until age 67. Those born before 1960 can begin to receive full benefits somewhere between ages 65 to 67, depending on their birth year.

Determining the right strategy for when to begin drawing Social Security should take some serious planning. Your individual life expectancy, your "full retirement age" as defined by Social Security, the anticipated value of your assets at the time of retirement need all be considered. Keep the following in mind while you deliberate your choices:

If you want to start collecting benefits before your "full retirement age" you may reduce your monthly benefit by as much as 30%. You can also delay taking benefits until age 70 if you want a larger benefit later in life.

Delaying your Social Security benefit payments means you will have to rely on your savings to fund the early years of your retirement. This could shrink your portfolio and reduce the returns you expect in later years. On the other hand, if you claim benefits early and unexpectedly outlast your savings you may end up living on a reduced Social Security benefit for the rest of your life.

If you plan to continue working, you can begin receiving benefits as soon as you reach your full retirement age.

Look Before You Leap!

The next critical issue in deciding your retirement age is medical insurance. Medicare will not be available (under most circumstances) until you reach age 65, regardless of whether you decide to take Social Security benefits at an earlier age. Please be clear about that fact because many people think Medicare will automatically kick in once Social Security does. No, you must be age 65. Let's say you can retire at age 62 and you currently have medical coverage on your employer's group insurance policy. Some companies have policies where you can continue coverage after you retire; most do not. Even if you can continue on the group policy, you may have to pay the full premium with no company contribution anymore and this can be a costly surprise.

If continuing coverage is not an option, your alternatives may be obtaining a "Cobra" policy which extends coverage for a maximum of 18 months from the date you leave the company employment, obtaining an individual medical policy or going uninsured until you reach age 65 for Medicare. You can expect to pay a hefty premium for this coverage.

Obtaining an individual medical policy is easier said than done for some. First, expect a pricey premium. You can bring down the premium cost by choosing an HMO program or using high deductibles. Health Savings Accounts, newly approved by Congress, can also help you save on medical expenses and we cover them in detail in a later chapter. Most importantly, you first must QUALIFY to be accepted for coverage. Health issues such as high blood pressure or headaches or allergies perhaps were not considered problematic when you were covered by the group policy, but they may create an increase in premium for an individual policy, or worse yet, make you uninsurable.

The last option, being uninsured, is really not viable. You do not want to jeopardize your health by not having affordable medical assistance if needed. You do not want to jeopardize your investment savings by not having medical insurance. The majority of bankruptcies in our country are due to medical expenses. Do not overlook this very important issue.

Lori and John, while still in the decision process, feel John will need to work for a company who provides a group medical policy until they both have reached age 65 to spare themselves that extra expense. The added benefit is that they will have a longer time before having to use their nest egg as well as John's being able to contribute longer to the company's 401-k plan.

6

Is Your State Tax Friendly?

While we spend much time focusing on federal income taxes and federal estate taxes when we are doing financial and estate planning, important consideration needs to be given to state taxes. It is more complicated as different states have different taxes. Some states will tax your personal income (for example, Nevada and Wyoming and Texas are some of the states that do not); your corporate income (not taxed in Wyoming); sales tax (Alaska has neither a sales tax nor a personal income tax). Rates on property taxes have large disparities between the states. We expect the state taxes to continue to be an important issue as most states are already working with a deficit budget and therefore need serious income. The mounting health-care and Medicaid costs are adding to the states' woes and the Feds can't come to the rescue as they have their own budget worries.

Bloomberg completed a recent study that compares the states, rating the best to the worst for retirement. The study is startling in its findings. A retiree this year that would owe $3,445 in taxes in Hawaii would owe $17,756 in Wisconsin! The same salary that generates a $54,211 tax bill in Vermont would only cost the taxpayer $9,483 in the next door state of New Hampshire.

Best States:

Wyoming
Nevada
Tennessee
Alabama
Alaska
Colorado
Washington
Louisiana

Delaware
Arizona

Worst States:

Rhode Island
Wisconsin
New York
Vermont
Nebraska
New Jersey
Maine
Idaho
Ohio
Oregon

One advantage of retirement is that you are freer to move than when you worked at a certain location. If you are not tied to a place by a paycheck, you can be open to explore different locales for agreeable climates, affordable housing costs, the availability of cultural and recreational facilities, proximity to family and friends—whatever issues are most important to us. We do recommend that you try renting in a new area before buying just to make sure the lifestyle is what you expect it to be. Relocating is expensive and requires energy, but if commensurate with your desires, so rewarding.

You can find detailed information about any state at www.bankrate.com/brm/itax/state/state

7

So You Want to Be in the Movies?

Okay, we have looked at some basic and logical actions that will help you retire sooner than later in the previous chapters. Now it's time for innovation so let's jump out of the box.

We have a client, Roxey, from Northern California, who has always loved horses and had owned one in her younger years. She wanted to retire from her profession which no longer gave her satisfaction but at age 61, she still needed income. After reviving her interest in horses by attending a number of equine shows, she came to us with her thoughts of buying a horse and giving riding lessons as her new endeavor. At first blush, we were cautious—while her rural home would accommodate horses and a training ring, there was the initial cost of about $20,000 coming out of her retirement savings to get the venture started. What swayed us was her passion, not just for horses, but the lifestyle she loved! As she said, she wasn't getting any younger and if she was going to enjoy horses in her life again, she better do it while the going was good! This initial vision set her on a course that several years later now includes: owning several horses, still giving riding lessons, training and breeding horses, having employees and most importantly, having work that adds joy to her life.

An inspiring story belongs to our friend Judy, in Arizona. At age 61 her spouse died after a very lengthy battle with cancer. Having been self employed, their individual policy for medical insurance was not the best. The ensuing medical bills plus having to care for her husband and not being able to work was devastating to their financial well-being. At a time when she had hoped to retire, she was faced with the loss of a spouse and mounting liabilities. Their lone salvageable asset was a note on a hotel which was in distress. Judy could have sold the note at a discounted basis but she elected to keep it and try to make the business profitable. Two years later, after many challenging 18 hour days, she has a viable business, a sense of accomplishment, and a valuable business she can now sell for a profit.

We mention these stories as it is important for us to realize that age or circumstances shouldn't limit our thinking. If we think we are too old to start over or to try something new, we aren't going to move forward. Do you love to dance? You could earn income as a dance instructor. With the Baby Boomers' demographics, there are lots of opportunities as that generation just keeps on kicking. Or, well, dancing! And it is physically great for your body too.

How about teaching something that interests you at your local community colleges? For many positions you do not need a BA, just substantiated experience in your line of endeavor. Many classes have twilight or evening schedules, so even if you can't leave your day job, you might earn something extra at night.

How about you golfers out there? Many golf clubs and courses have positions available—you don't have to be a pro! Earn some money for your retirement savings plus play free or at a discount rate when you want to enjoy the game.

If you enjoy traveling, you can mitigate some of your costs by renting out your home while you are gone or exchanging your home with other travelers. There are numerous agencies which put these packages together.

Have you always wanted to be in the movies? If you live in the Los Angeles, Las Vegas or New York area, no matter what your age or looks, you can be an "extra". My friend of many years, Tina, was looking for post retirement adventure and has been in more movies and TV shows than I can count. While the pay is minimum wage, her tales of the rich and famous personalities make for interesting conversation. Once you get on a studio's call list, you can be kept pretty busy, and entertained!

Do you think you should be more physically active? Do your body that favor and make some extra money by working at a gym. I know that often trainers at gyms are a size four and in their 20s, but there are other opportunities. For women in particular, there are gyms like "Curves" who market to middle-aged women and often staff mature women as their trainers. It's a concept that works—Curves is the largest growing franchise in the US at the time of this writing. I am a member and use their facilities while we travel the country so I personally can recommend this tactic as beneficial to both your pocketbook and your fitness.

Have you ever wondered who thought up that vegetable chopper on TV that can do everything but cook dinner? Well, some individual with more time on his (her) hands than seemingly good sense has made a lot of money with that invention. But in reality, we have several clients who do have patents or royalties. While some are sophisticated, one of our wealthier clients has a patent similar to a shoe polish to clean sneakers that is distributed by the large discount chains. Something simple can do the trick!

If you are serious about an idea of yours, you must think of the idea as business property, what is more frequently referred to now as intellectual property. Ideas are relatively easy to come by but inventions are more difficult. It takes knowledge and effort to refine an idea into workable invention, even on paper. Turning an invention into a new product accepted by the marketplace takes a lot of effort and overcoming substantial barriers in the path of those who pursue innovation.

Hundreds of thousands of inventions and innovators file each year for protection under trademark, patent and copyright laws. However, it can be hard to decide which of the three is most appropriate for the protection of a particular invention. To get specific information, do a search on the internet for "patents." There are numerous "how to" sites as well as companies that can take you through the entire patent process. For some, it can pay off quite well.

We encourage you to think outside of the box not only because of money issues but to make your retirement a time of enjoyment for you. We all know family or friends who retire only to think and act old and thereby become old. Don't cheat yourself!

Keep reading as we continue the discussion of how to cultivate a life of activity and interest and fun. You deserve it!

8

Accumulate Assets with Little Investment!

Yes, it can be done and we will devote a number of chapters to showing you proven techniques to help you with this strategy.

Let's begin with what might interest you. While we usually can do most of what it takes to survive and thrive, we do it better, and more easily, if we are involved in a subject that we find engaging or exciting.

Are you a handy person around the house? Are you an avid reader? Do you understand much about the construction business? Are your computer skills good? Do you enjoy decorating or designing? Is traveling part of your retirement goals? Do you enjoy garage sales? Have you invented things in your head? Do you like people and tend to be social? What are your hobbies? Do you enjoy bargain shopping? Do you have a green thumb? Are you a techie? Are you good at floral arrangements?

If you already have sufficient assets to get you through your retirement years you probably wouldn't be reading this book. So, we will assume you need to increase your nest egg any way you can and that may include some changes to your current routine. Hey, this should be looked at as a growing opportunity! What you have done in the past may not be working so let's roll up our sleeves and create wealth.

A Favorite!

One of our favorite (and tested by ourselves) opportunities is buying a home that is a "fixer-upper," fix it up while you live in it, then sell it at a profit. Let's start with why this is a good idea. Current tax law allows us to buy our personal residence, live in it for a minimum of two years out of the past five years and then sell it with the profits of up to $250,000.00 per person (or $500,000.00 for a married couple) to be excluded from any capital gains tax. This is huge!

There are some guidelines to help this process be a profitable one. You want to purchase a fixer-upper that is below the average listed price of homes in the neighborhood, remembering that you will have remodeling costs to add to your eventual selling price. If you are not knowledgeable about construction, you can attend classes at stores like Home Depot or some community colleges for construction how-to and remodeling ideas. Talk with experienced realtors about what brings value to houses in your part of the country. For example, installing a pool in most cases is not beneficial but having decent landscaping in both the front and back yard is important. Adding a bathroom will often increase value over adding another bedroom. Updating kitchen appliances usually is a good idea but turning a garage into an extra bedroom or office is not. Often it is the small items that give the biggest returns in resale such as new faucets and door handles which help to modernize a house. Take down old curtains (including shower curtains) and throw away old welcoming mats. If you are not installing new carpeting, make sure what you have is clean, clean, clean! Fresh looking paint, both interior and exterior will give a home a well maintained look. And keep the paint colors neutral! Once you retire you can have your forest green dining room walls but for this venture, you need to appeal to the masses. Often your best returns are on cosmetic type improvements as opposed to structural changes. You get to live in the house while you complete improvements as your energy and cash flow allows. This also provides you with the flexibility of selling when you choose, i.e., when the market is good. Remember the house must be your main residence for a two year period, but you can do this over and over again every two years.

If moving your personal residence every few years does not appeal to you, there are other real estate venues that can create wealth. The first we'll discuss is obtaining property by foreclosure.

Foreclosures

There are numerous seminars and books that deal with the subject of real estate foreclosures. While we speak in generalities, keep in mind that state laws dictate the rules so what might work in one state may not in the next. While opportunities do exist to make money in this field, you should have competent legal advice to keep yourself out of trouble. There are four basic levels of foreclosure:

Buying from owners behind on their mortgage payments
Buying from owners who have had a notice of default filed against them
Buying property at the foreclosure sale, which is often an auction
Buying property from the lender who recovered the foreclosed property

It's hard to find people in the first category although success at that level can be rewarding. The trick is finding these people—there aren't lists for the public of people who owe two or three months of back mortgage. People who deal at this level often use billboards and/or newspaper adds saying "we will buy your home immediately." The home owners may want to save their credit rating via a quick sale rather than have a typical escrow time; they may have hoped for other alternatives that didn't work and realize they are running out of time; sometimes people will sign over a quitclaim deed for moving expenses and some cash for a quick new start. These dealings are not for the faint of heart although it can be argued that in some cases, an owner getting something instead of nothing is a better alternative. One caution—quit claim deeds, by which a seller can assign title to the buyer, can give you some very unpleasant surprises. A quit claim deed assigns the property immediately to the buyer, but it is subject to any liens, mortgages, taxes, and judgments that exist against the property. The buyer should protect himself by having a title search completed and obtain title insurance prior to a quit claim deed being executed.

The next level, owners who have had a notice of default filed, are a matter of public record and there are numerous companies who publish these lists. Which means, of course, there is plenty of competition for the homeowner to choose from. Negotiating may take more skill and more money at this level.

If you wish to be a buyer at the foreclosure auction or sale (again, state laws rule!) you normally would need the cash amount of your bid in a cashier's check to pay off the current lender. If there is more than one mortgage on the property, the second or third mortgage holders will most likely be bidding against you for the property. This level obviously requires more capital in order to participate.

Lastly, there is buying the property from a lending institution that has it in it's REO (Real Estate Owned) department. Depending on the size of the institution, they may be excited to get the property off their books or they may automatically turn it over to a real estate broker for disposal. Get to know your banker and find out the particulars of their REOs—it could be a worthy project.

Foreclosures can be money makers but it takes time, knowledge of the laws and working the numbers. To do it profitably, one must be able to devote time and energy to it, so keep that in mind before you sign up for one of those real estate "how to" seminars!

BE A Middleman!

Are you a person who enjoys shopping? Garage sales? Antique hunting? Do you own a retail business that needs a marketing boost? Your efforts can very likely be rewarded if you choose to be a middleman, offering items for sale on the internet. We were wary during our early investigations of Ebay and other internet auction sites, but we have become believers, now personally having purchased a number of things ourselves and being very satisfied with the transactions. Apparently some companies will hold a portion of their inventory, all new, to sell on Ebay at a lesser cost than retail. We have purchased radio remote broadcasting equipment, business office telephone equipment, digital cameras, golf clubs, and several software programs at discounted rates and, when sold new, they came with the warranties and registrations just as if we had purchased them at a store. We even listed for rent our home on the golf course in San Diego for Super Bowl week 2002 between the Raiders and the Bucs.

Ebay estimates that about 145,000 entrepreneurs make a full time living selling their wares through the service. Thousands of small sellers move astonishing arrays of items each hour. You can get a quick look at the diversity by glancing at Ebay's opening page or enter a word in the search box. Type in "jam" and you'll get back over 5,000 items. The auction service employs over 5,000 people. While items like auto parts, collector items, trading cards, books, golf clubs, artwork, clothing, CDs, toys, computers, and software might come to mind when thinking about internet auctions, there is a trend for more established businesses, large and small, to enter the fray offering a multitude of items—19 ton process chillers for computer rooms, heavy construction equipment and automobiles. The theme seems to be if there is a seller, there also is a buyer!

Part of the mechanics of settling the "buy" is often done through PayPal. If you win an auction, you can send the seller payment within minutes. And it is secure in that the seller never sees the buyer's credit card numbers. If you are buying big ticket items, such as works of art, where fraud might be a concern, you can go to escrow.com, which holds money until the goods have been delivered and inspected.

Readers! Read Up!

Are you an avid reader? People who love to read often have secret longings to author a great American novel. We know because we do! Consider the story of J.K. Rowling, who was divorced, living on public assistance with an infant daughter, and who against all odds wrote the Harry Potter novels and skyrocketed to fame, fortune and the satisfaction of having done a spectacular job. The ideal route of course, is to write the novel, be published and sell millions of copies. There are, however, other ways to accomplish profitable authorship. Are you a specialist in a field, be it technical, creative, business, history, motivation? Advice or the how to books can be quite successful. People also use books to market their businesses as a published author helps brand a person as an expert in their field. This aura of authority can boost marketing and sales. Whether you are a creator of the great novel or an expert-turned-author, you can use self-publishing resources. These companies are web based or the traditional print operations, usually offering graphic design, layout, editing as well as printing. Most will offer assistance with copyright and sales and distribution through traditional or online booksellers. Prices vary but it is possible to be "published" for less than a $1,000.00.

Some service providers are Xlibris.com (888)795-4274; iUniverse.com (800)376-1736; Fidlar Doubleday (800)248-0888; Cameo Publications (843) 785-3770; Express Media (615) 360-6400.

Real Estate Exchanges

Do you own any property that is not your residence? Whether is it vacant land or a property that provides you with income this may be a way to maximize your returns on it. There is a new IRS Reg 2002-22, which allows a 1031 Exchange with expanded options. What is a 1031 Exchange? A rule that allows a property owner to sell their current property and exchange it for another of like kind with no gain or loss recognized. The new Reg 2002-22 allows an expansion of what can be considered like kind.

What is "like-kind"? Rental houses, condominiums, apartment buildings, shopping centers, warehouses, office buildings, vacant land, farm land. You can exchange any of these types of real estate or another—vacant land or an office building and so forth. What can you NOT exchange into? Bonds, securities, notes, and property outside of the U.S.

The new Reg 2002-22 allows for Tenant in Common Interests when purchasing the exchange property. A simple example is this: A couple have $500,000 equity in farm property that they sell; they take their $500,000 equity and combine it with other sellers, who each own their share of the new property as a Tenant In Common. This Tenant in Common procedure allows investment in a single property by multiple owners, not in a partnership or other entity, but as individual owners. Each owner receives a deed at closing; each owner has an undivided percentage interest in the entire property; and all benefits and obligations will be shared by the tenants in common in proportion to their respective undivided interests in the property. There are a number of professional real estate companies who specialize in this, such as Wells Real Estate, who manage over $3 Billion of real estate assets, and Inland Real Estate out of Chicago who manage over $5 Billion of real estate assets. By purchasing sizable buildings, leases can be made to companies of net worth exceeding $100 million, such at IBM, BellSouth, General Electric. The triple net leases usually require the tenant to pay taxes, maintenance, insurance, and improvements in addition to their rent. The professional property management expertise enables the project to maximize profitability and have cash available for distribution to investors. The contracts we have seen often have quarterly distributions and are set for a 7% annual return. In addition, the owners are able to write off depreciation and may enjoy property appreciation at the end of lease term, typically ten years. Such terms and conditions of course can be different for different properties.

What are the requirements to defer taxes on a sale under Section 1031? The purchase of property of equal or greater value with equal or greater debt. When single sellers combine with other sellers this option is not a problem.

These Tenant in Common projects might be appropriate for anyone who owns real estate investments, but especially for owners with highly appreciated property, or owners who are tired of the headaches of being a landlord, i.e., dealing with tenants, maintaining properties, paying taxes, and so forth; those who want to eliminate landlord duties and still receive cash flow from property ownership;

investors seeking real estate diversification; and investors who might own vacant land or property not paying a cash flow who desire cash income.

If you are interested, you can contact a securities broker as shares are available only through people who are securities licensed.

9

Tax Lien Certificates!

This chapter continues with the theme of accumulating assets with little investment and we feel this topic deserves a chapter of its own.

What are tax lien certificates?

When a property owner does not pay the property taxes and the county, needing the funds to continue to operate the county expenses, places a first lien on the property for the amount of the unpaid taxes plus interest and penalties, if any. The county then offers the tax lien to the public for purchase via a bidding process. In Arizona, the interest rate for certificates begins at 16% goes to the lowest bidder; in Florida the bidding starts at 18%.

Why haven't I heard about them?

Tax Lien Certificates have been in existence for decades, but only about 25 states offer them, with Arizona, Florida, Colorado, and Illinois being some of the more popular ones. The states that do not offer Tax Lien Certificates, such as California, are known as tax deed states and handle tax delinquencies differently. Other states, such as Texas and Georgia, offer a hybrid known as redeemable deeds.

Seven Reasons to Consider Purchasing Tax Lien Certificates:

They are government issued.

They are a first lien on the property, even before any mortgages.

Potential high levels of interest return. The bidding maximum in Arizona is 16%; in Florida it is 18%.

Real estate has a low correlation to stock and bond investments and provides diversification to one's estate.

A Tax Lien Certificate holder may have an opportunity to end up with valuable real estate as a bonus.

Collections of the taxes and payments to the investor are handled by the County Treasurer's Office. When a tax lien certificate is redeemed, the County sends principal and interest directly to the investor. There is no need for interaction with the property owner.

Normally a small amount of cash is needed to acquire a tax lien position on a particular property.

In states where tax lien certificates are issued by government entities, the purchase of a tax lien certificate is more secure than a first mortgage on property, and carries with it a high interest rate of return. *It is not a purchase of the property.*

Because we are familiar with the Arizona Tax Lien Certificate process, we shall use that state for explaining in detail the process. Each state and county will have its own particular way of handling the Tax Lien Certificate sales, so you will want to research well before jumping in!

Prior to the sale, in the state of Arizona, the tax collector advertises the delinquent taxes in a local newspaper and on the internet. At the auction, the Treasurer takes bids starting at 16%. Tax certificates not sold to private bidders at the annual sale are available for purchase by private purchasers and their representatives and returns the full 16% rate.

Bidders, or their representatives, should do extensive research on each property they believe may be deserving of their bidding. Purchases of tax liens do not result in an inflow of cash until they are redeemed by the owner of the property. However, cashing out is possible where another purchaser is found to purchase the certificate.

UP-SIDE RISKS:

1. Arizona Tax Lien Certificates can be high yielding investments.

No discussion of the risks inherent in Arizona tax liens would be complete if it did not reference the existence of the substantial "up-side risk" of owning the Tax Lien Certificates (TLCs). Since the TLC is given statutory priority over consensual mortgage liens, even first mortgages or first deeds of trusts on the property, it is more secure than those liens. With interest rates paid on TLCs upon redemption by the owner at a statutory maximum of 16%, and historic "as purchased" averages in the double digits, there is no denying the fact that in the current economic climate the investment return is quite high compared to most other investments. Arizona TLCs are mostly redeemed by the property owner within a couple of years, if not much sooner.

If a property owner does not redeem within three years from the auction date where the TLC was purchased, the holder of the TLC can foreclose on the TLC by utilizing a procedure known as judicial foreclosure, a civil lawsuit with many of the same features as are present in Arizona judicial foreclosure of consensual mortgages which are in default. A hypothetical TLC buyer may have paid $1,000.00 for the TLC, and after three years from the auction date, pay attorneys' fees and court costs for the foreclosure on a property which may have a value of many times the total amount expended by the investor. As is sometimes the case in conventional real estate purchase transactions, real property ownership through foreclosure of unredeemed TLCs is not necessarily a positive. Down-side risks of such real estate ownership will be discussed in later paragraphs of this letter.

DOWN-SIDE RISKS

1. Bankruptcy, although it is not supposed to "affect security," can have a negative affect on TLCs.

Since the particular county treasurer selling the TLC will have determined there is not a bankruptcy pending prior to the auction sale, these issues arise only after the investor has bought the TLC and the defaulting owner has later filed for bankruptcy, either before or after the expiration of three years from the date of the purchase of the TLC at the auction, which time period is the Arizona required waiting time before the investor's right to foreclose on the unredeemed TLC matures.

Although a TLC is secured by a lien on the particular property on which it is issued, a bankruptcy by the owner of the property can a.) stop or slow down the process of foreclosure on the lien, b.) result in elimination or decrease in the interest rate to be paid by the redeeming owner, or, c.) in the worst case, result in a discharge of the property tax obligation, eliminating the validity of the lien on the property and resulting in the TLC investor losing its investment on that lien.

a.) Affect on pending or future foreclosure.

A TLC investor who has brought a judicial foreclosure in Arizona may find his state court action stayed by the automatic stay of the bankruptcy court when the defaulting owner files for bankruptcy protection. Usually, but not always, the stay will be lifted upon appropriate motion by the investor's attorney, to allow the foreclosure of the tax lien (a secured debt which is not supposed to be affected by bankruptcy, in theory, but not always in practice) to proceed in state court.

Similarly, an investor who finds the defaulting owner has filed for bankruptcy prior to the expiration of three years from the auction date at which the TLC was acquired, must proceed in the bankruptcy court for an order to lift the stay when the three years have expired, or simply wait for the conclusion of the bankruptcy case, at which time judicial foreclosure can be instituted without an order of the bankruptcy court lifting the stay (which ends when the bankruptcy case ends, usually with a discharge of all unsecured debts, in a Chapter 7 liquidation bankruptcy proceeding).

b.) Possible elimination or decrease in the interest rate to be paid by the redeeming owner.

The possibility of elimination or decrease in the TLC interest rate could generally take place in the context of Chapter 13 (reorganization of wage earner) Plans approved by a judge who has weighed the equities of affecting the right of investors to get paid on their TLCs at the rate provided by law and understood by the investor to be its entitlement, or, alternatively, at the rate, and at the pace, which a wage earner can afford to pay in order to enable him or her to get back on his or her feet, which a judge could find to be a minimal rate and a longer period than the three years waiting period required to bring a judicial foreclosure action, in order to effectuate the Chapter 13 Plan for reorganization of the debtor's financial affairs.

c.) Worst case discharge of the tax lien obligation.

The discharge of the tax lien could take place when a trustee has moved the bankruptcy court to subordinate the lien to his and his attorney's fees which are classified as administration expenses in the bankruptcy proceeding, which in a minority of cases, would result in the TLC being rendered an unsecured priority claim, with the practical effect of the investor getting a reduced amount or, in the worst case, nothing.

2. Underground Storage Tanks or other environmental hazard may render the underlying property a liability to its record owner or, for other reasons the real estate's value may not exceed the value of the tax lien.

Typically, the owner of Arizona real estate is held responsible for environmental hazards found on it, even if the owner has no knowledge of the hazards. Cleaning up these hazards may not be economically feasible and liability for harm caused by them could amount to far more money than the property is worth. In the event the investor chooses to foreclose, after waiting the three years from the date of auction, and assuming the foreclosure goes to judgment declaring the investor to be the new owner, the investor inherits any environmental worries whether they be obvious or hidden, which is not unlike acquiring a loathsome disease from a new lover, one thought to be pure as the driven snow.

Precautions can be taken by an investor or its representatives in advance of acquiring the TLC or, ultimately, the title to the property through foreclosure. First, properties used as gas stations or oil change depots can be spotted by a visual drive by of the property and are usually obvious from county assessor records (made available on the internet several of the urban Arizona counties, such as Maricopa-Phoenix Metro area). Even the name of the record owner of the property up for bid at the auction may tell a potential investor or its representative all they need to know about the use made of the property.

Generally, special care should be made when it is ascertained that a particular tax lien is being offered for sale on property of a commercial or retail nature. Residential properties, although perhaps not quite as likely to have environmental hazards upon them, could reveal other concerns, such as public or private nuisance related ones, from a drive by of the property. Sometimes, there are neighborhoods, subdivisions or perhaps entire small towns which are known to be in an area which has more potential for these types of problems and therefore best for the investor to pass on tax liens offered on those properties within those areas.

The Arizona Department of Environmental Quality (ADEQ) keeps lists on environmentally hazardous properties and should be consulted as a preventative measure to alleviate a percentage of the risk.

Similarly blighted areas of a county or town would properly be avoided by an investor or its representative where the lack of desirability of a property could likely affect its prospects for future redemption by the defaulting owner or for sale at a sufficient price by an investor who has chosen to foreclose after the period for redemption expires.

3. Liquidity of the TLC investment.

Investors do not know when a TLC will be redeemed. It could be that a hypothetical TLC would be redeemed during the first month after the TLC is purchased, most likely by a property owner who is normally conscientious but has fallen behind temporarily due to any number of factors, such as loss of a job. The TLC may never be redeemed, necessitating foreclosure if the investor determines that to be the prudent course of action. On the other hand, the TLC could be redeemed in eighteen months from the date it was purchased, a more or less average amount of time for redemption.

Obviously, the investor has no way of knowing when it will get its money back to spend on something else or to reinvest. This can be alleviated somewhat through a process of "laddering" TLC investments by purchasing a number of them at any given auction, which will then allow the law of averages to assist in providing a form of cash flow over the subsequent months and years, as every now and then the chances are that one, although it is not known which one, of the TLCs will be redeemed.

While a successful judicial foreclosure will result in the court's Judgment of foreclosure and will be followed by the issuance of the treasurer's deed to the property, any hesitancy by title agencies to insure the title may affect future sale of the property, causing an increase in the lack of the liquidity of the investor's investment.

4. Bureaucratic incompetence or administrative errors.

In Arizona, Maricopa County (Phoenix Metro) is fairly well automated and computerized but some of the outlying counties, such as Cochise County are not particularly tech savvy. Even in Maricopa, mistakes do happen. However, Maricopa's policy of paperless TLCs which are evidenced by a hard copy receipt and then followed by regular periodic accountings, automatically issued, and ultimately followed by checks automatically generated to the investor and sent by the Treasurer upon receipt by it of the redemption funds by the owner, make efficient and accurate TLC transactions far more likely than not. Other counties, some of which depend upon the investor responding to a notice of redemption before cutting a check for the redeemed funds, are much less "fool proof."

Usually, a county treasurer whose office has erred will be more than happy to see to it that the error is remedied promptly, but unless the transactions with the treasurer are monitored constantly by the investor, an error could occur to the investor's detriment which may go unnoticed for years, or perhaps never noticed at all. When such errors occur and an investor has suffered some monetary damage, the Arizona statutes provide a basis for relief.

Other errors, which can usually be corrected, include the offering of a TLC by the treasurer on a property which is owned by the government or a charity, property which is normally exempt from property tax. Also, although the treasurer will usually check to see if a bankruptcy has been filed by the property owner in default before offering a TLC for sale, sometimes properties subject to the bankruptcy court's automatic stay against any transfers (including selling of liens) will slip through the cracks. When this is discovered, the treasurer will of course refund the TLC purchase price, but without receiving interest on its investment, the investor's overall yield on its portfolio of TLCs will be reduced.

Changes in the Arizona statutes, just as unpredictable as the liquidity of the TLCs themselves, may make it more or less difficult in the future to invest in TLCs, on any number of fronts. For instance, if the State Legislature were to decide that its statutory maximum interest rate of 16% should be reduced for whatever reason it need simply reduce the amount which is now provided by law to be 16%. It is unimaginable that such a reduction could be made to be retroactive to TLCs already purchased but it could conceivably affect the yield of the investor when it seeks to purchase the TLCs for subsequent taxes on a property on which it already holds a TLC[1].

See the book, "Arizona Property Tax Liens, Guide to Profit, Protection and Prosecution," by Mark L. Manoil for more details. Website: www.taxsalelists.com.

A CASE IN POINT—MARICOPA COUNTY, ARIZONA

This is the way the Maricopa County (Phoenix) Treasurer's Office described the process of the 2003 auction for acquiring tax liens in Phoenix, Arizona, which has its auctions conducted by every county treasurer's office in the state for from 1-4 days (depending on the county) during the month of February each year:

---

1.   Current law specifies that the interest yielded on amounts paid by an investor for subsequent taxes is the same interest amount to be paid on the initial TLC purchased by the investor. A.R.S. §42-18153

AUCTION

The Tax Lien Sale provides for the payment of delinquent property taxes by an investor. The tax on the property is auctioned in open competitive bidding based on the least percent of interest to be received by the investor.

Property taxes that are delinquent at the end of December are added to any previously uncollected taxes on a parcel for the Tax Lien Sale. The sale takes place in February of each year. Please read the disclaimer before deciding to bid, and see our lien FAQ page and lien history page.

Parcels whose taxes are subject to sale, will be advertised, in January, in a Maricopa County newspaper of general circulation. They are listed by parcel number and have a sequence number for bidding purposes. The advertisement appears about three weeks before the auction. Copies of the newspaper are usually available for purchase at Treasurer's Office. In addition, a diskette and CD of those parcels can also be purchased.

The investor is responsible for all research on the parcels available for auction. County maps for research may be obtained by visiting the Maricopa County Assessor's Office. Read our Recommendations to all bidders.

PRE-SALE REQUIREMENTS

To be eligible to bid, investors must provide the Treasurer's Office with a completed Bidder Information Card and Request for Taxpayer Identification Number and Certification (Form W-9). These may be obtained in the Client Services Department. A number will be assigned to each bidder for use when purchasing tax liens.

BID PROCEDURE

The sequence number and the amount will be read in the order they appear in the newspaper. Visual bids will be recognized as interest rates are called. The lowest interest rate bid on a parcel will be awarded the lien or Certificate of Purchase (CP). Bidders must be present. Bids by telephone or mail are not accepted.

The successful bidder will pay the entire amount of taxes, interest, and fees with guaranteed funds by the end of the next day. If payment has not been made the parcel(s) may be re-offered.

The sale will continue until all liens are sold or the lack of bidding warrants discontinuing the sale.

Each investor will receive an Unmatured Portfolio Report identifying each parcel for which the investor had acquired a tax lien. When making an inquiry on a property, use the parcel number located in the left column of the Portfolio.

BID INTEREST

Bids must be on the basis of interest income to bidder.

1. The maximum bid is 16% simple interest per annum, prorated monthly. The lowest acceptable bid is 0% per annum.

2. The successful (lowest) bid will determine the rate of interest to be paid on the Tax Lien, representing the amount of taxes, interest, fees and charges then due.

REDEMPTION OF LIENS

If the owner and/or agent redeems the property, the investor receives a payment of what they paid for the lien, less the processing fee, plus the prorated monthly rate of interest that was awarded at the sale.

DEEDS

When a property owner fails to redeem the CP prior to the expiration of three years from the date the parcel was first offered at sale, the investor may apply for a court ordered deed to the property (judicial foreclosure). The Treasurer does not participate in judicial foreclosures. A Treasurer's Deed may be applied for after five years from the date of sale. The last day to apply for a Treasurer's Deed is December 31, 2003. After that date all foreclosures must be judicial.

ASSIGNMENTS

Assignments offer the investor an alternative way to purchase liens on parcels at a time other then the Tax Lien sale.

The unsold parcels "struck off to state" (State CPs) at the Tax Lien sale are available to investors by assignment. Assignments will be available upon completion of all Sale Week transactions. Assignment purchases may be made in person or by mail. Payment must accompany the request.

Available parcels are listed as "STATE CP" on a printout located in the Client Services Department of the Treasurer's Office. This listing is available for purchase in two forms, printout or diskette, for $50 each. It lists the tax amount and year involved. The buyer will pay the entire amount of taxes, interest, and fees due at the date of the assignment. The final date for purchasing assignments is January 31. The remaining assignments are prepared for the Tax Lien Sale in February.

NOTE: If a parcel also has current delinquent taxes in addition to "State CP" taxes, the investor may purchase both after June 1, and prevent the parcel from going to the Tax Lien Sale.

ASSIGNMENT PURCHASING

The buyer will submit a list of desired parcels to the Treasurer's Office, along with a cashier's check, money order, certified check, or wire transfer for the approximate total. The submittals will be recorded and processed in the order in which they are received. Should the original payment be in excess of the amount due, a refund will be issued.

The calculations will be made on the assignments up to the amount received. Parcels not covered by funds on hand, must remain available to other buyers. The interest earned on an assignment will be the current statutory maximum (16%).

"Assignment" must be specified to prevent an inadvertent processing of a redemption of a Certificate of Purchase.

SUBTAX

Subsequent Tax (Subtax) can be added to an existing lien to protect the investor's fiduciary interest. The subtaxing of the current year's taxes onto existing lien begins June 1 and ends January 31. All remaining taxes go to the Tax Lien Sale in February.

The investor is responsible for the research of the parcel's unpaid taxes. The subtax consists of taxes, interest, and fees dependent on the date the taxes are being paid. There is an additional $5.00 fee for each purchase submitted for subtax to be applied for each year requested.

The payment procedure for a subtax is the same as for assignments. The interest earned on a subtax is the same as that of the original CP.

TRANSFER OF CERTIFICATES OF PURCHASE

If not redeemed, a CP may be transferred by affidavit to another person who has a Bidder Identification Card on file with the Treasurer's Office. There is a $10.00 transfer fee. <u>The Treasurer's Office must be notified of the transfer for it to be valid.</u> The Treasurer pays the redeemed taxes to the last CP holder on record.

MONTHLY ACTIVITY STATEMENT

An Activity Statement will be sent to each CP buyer listing their redemptions, purchases, and surrenders. Statements will not be sent for those accounts that have not had activity.

In February of both years, we attended the Maricopa County (Phoenix) 2003 and 2004 auctions, where the delinquent tax year 2001and 2002 tax lien certificates (TLCs) were sold. Very productive! Also, very well attended by buyers who were all after one thing—a yield in excess of the less than 2% they could get from more conventional investments, i.e. bank CDs, etc.

In fact, the TLCs were going for well into the double digits on the average. Now, with many of the TLCs offered but unsold at the public auction, there are 27,000 left over which are now for sale over the counter, **all at 16%, the maximum allowed by law**. Not all of these OTC TLCs (I apologize for all of the acronyms) are worth buying. Forget about buying a TLC for taxes which are under $250—they just usually are not worth the effort. But there is plenty of high quality product left over from the auction from which to choose. These are now all on our data base. The sooner the selections are made the more likely these TLCs will be close to the quality of the TLCs purchased through competitive bidding at the auction.

Why would we be interested in TLCs that were not bid on at the auction? Imagine 1,000 tax lien certificates being sold each hour! How fast did the auctioneer have to go to get through the list of 40,000 plus TLCs on sale in Phoenix? Well, try about one every 4 seconds! Maybe you can begin to see how quality TLCs have been overlooked by the bidders who were moving at warp speed during the auction.

10

Accumulate Income with a Little Effort

Perhaps you are close to retiring from your career job, or have already retired and still need to earn a wage. It is important to know there are opportunities that lend themselves to middle aged people better than others. Yes, we know that hiring practices are supposed to be age blind but we also know that is not always the case.

I am quite a shopper but I haven't seen many middle aged salespeople in some of the more popular boutique stores. However, go into the department stores and the mature employees will be visible. We salute Home Depot for its initiative in seeking the experienced (in life) employee in its employment practices. There aren't too many 65 year old men dressed in orange shorts serving spicy chicken wings at Hooters Restaurants, although with the large number of single/widowed female retirees, it might be a good marketing angle! The important thing is that if you are job searching you need to know there are opportunities out there.

Real estate sales, for example, has countless examples of mature top producers. It is a demanding profession, yet one that welcomes people from all walks of life. You need to become licensed by the state but there are excellent schools to get you qualified. Many of the larger real estate franchises have additional educational classes for their agents to see them through the licensing and learning the business practices.

We will share a story with you about Donna, a very good fiend of ours. In her mid fifties, she found herself newly divorced, faced with starting over. Due to a failed business of her ex-husband's, she had few assets at a time in her life when she had hoped to kick back and enjoy. The change from married to divorced and from having been somewhat financially secure to worrying about how to make ends meet created an emotional and social upheaval in her life.

California was in a real estate recession at the time, but she chose to enter the field again as she had worked in it in her early career days. It wasn't quite like riding a bicycle, however, as forms and practices had changed a lot over the years. I remember her telling us how she dreaded Fridays, because on Friday she called all the people who had listed homes with her to report on the week's activities. During that recession, there was little activity. It was extremely difficult for people who had to sell because there were few to no buyers out there and some people still like to blame the messenger for bringing bad news.

It was a tough time but Donna kept at it. That tenacity paid off royally as not only did she become the leading sales person in the area, she met a wonderful man, John, whom she married. Now their days are spent traveling and golfing. You must never give up as opportunities could be right around the corner for you.

A newer profession is the sales of Long Term Care Insurance. As it is a relatively new product the employment opportunities are good. And since the buyers of Long Term Care are typically 50+, the middle-aged salesperson might more easily connect with them. While long term care insurance policies will vary greatly from carrier to carrier, the basic tenets are easily learned. Most states require that you obtain a life license in order to sell the insurance.

Pull Your Own Red Wagon!

Are you are a closet entrepreneur, ready now to leap into your own business? Does Bridal Consultant, Child Care Services, Catering, Gift Basket Services, Cleaning Services, Matchmaking Services, Medical Claims Billings, Floral Arranging or Computer Consultant interest you? In a sign of what retirement in the U.S. might look like in the coming decades, a new study shows that a growing share of older workers are starting their own businesses. We examine network marketing opportunities in detail in Chapter Eleven.

One research study, released June 5, 2004, was conducted for AARP by Rand Corporation, a think tank in California. About 16% of our nation's workers who are at least 50 years old, or 5.6 million people, were self-employed in 2002. While the percentage is off slightly from 1998, it still is higher than the 10% self-employment level of the overall work force, which counts for 13.8 million people in business for themselves. Consequently, the 50-plus workers account for 40% of all people in business for themselves. The number of self-employed older people has been inching up for several years, even as the overall number of self-employed Americans has declined. It is a trend that is expected to continue.

If you are thinking about joining this parade of business owners, there are things you need to consider to give yourself the best chances of success. First, you need to select your company name. It ideally will identify the type of service/products you provide or simply tout the name of the founder. A wise man, my husband David, advises that the "identification" aspect is a most important marketing tool for you. Acme Enterprises will leave people scratching their head or even worse, easily forgetting the name as it doesn't relate to anything. Roxburgh's New Home Marketing, on the other hand, lets everyone know immediately what you do and what your name is!

You next need to select a business structure, such as a sole proprietorship, a "C" corporation, an "S" corporation, or an LLC. The LLC is not a corporation but it offers many of the same advantages, combining the limited liability of a corporation with the "pass through" taxation of a sole proprietorship. Some fledgling companies will begin as an LLC and make a change to a corporate structure for tax or other reasons once they are established. If you do decide to incorporate, research the best state for it. Many business owners automatically do so in the state where they plan to operate because it often seems less complicated. However, Delaware holds appeal for new companies for its low incorporation fees and franchise taxes. Likewise, Nevada is becoming increasingly business friendly with its advantageous tax structure.

Home Based Businesses

If you are planning to run your business from home, be sure to check with your local zoning board or government office for the rules in your town. If you are living in a planned community or condominium, also check to see whether any rules or deed restrictions limit the commercial use of your property.

While some very successful people started out by working from their kitchen table, if you are making a serious commitment towards a profitable venture, you want to consider some small things that will help you. Good lighting, desk space that doesn't do dual duty with other family members, a comfortable chair and enough file cabinet space to allow you to get and remain organized. A place for everything and everything in its place is good advice to keep you sane. Even if you have the space to take a spare bedroom and lock yourself in, an office in the home will have lots of distractions.

In today's world, a computer is a must and you can get a great set-up for $1,000 or less. Fax machines make life easier and many of them now are a combination fax and printer. Even if you have Kinko's or another copier shop close to your location, having a printer in house will make your tasks easier. Phones are another item you do not want to share with the family. Your own business phone produces a more professional image, it automatically provides a telephone listing in the white pages and you won't miss important calls while your daughter is on the phone with a friend.

The Wall Street Journal has a special section for entrepreneurs at WSJ.com which is loaded with important information.

Buying a Franchise

Maybe starting something from scratch does not appeal to you. Every year thousands of entrepreneurs wrestle with the decision to go it alone or perhaps buy a franchise.

A franchise is a legal and commercial relationship between the owner of a trademark, trade name, or advertising symbol and an individual or group that wish to use that business identity. A quality franchisor will provide their franchisees with a good product or service to sell; employee training; assistance with marketing and finance; site location and so on. For these services, there will be an initial franchise fee to pay as well as a sharing of your profits on a continuing basis.

Because franchises are technically a partnership, you want to be very careful before signing the contract and handing over your money. Besides doing the regular due diligence regarding the franchisor's financial health, we recommend you speak with a number of other franchisees in the system to learn of their experiences. Just as importantly, seeing an attorney to make sure you understand exactly what you are committing to and the legal status of the franchise could save you future headaches. To find lawyers who specialize in this industry, go to aafd.org, the website of the American Association of Franchisees and Dealers or the American Franchisee Association. For additional information, go to the WSJ.com franchise section mentioned earlier. If you wish to use a franchise broker, try the websites FranNet.com and FranChoice.com.

Because franchises take serious capital investments, you may find a network marketing independent distributorship, which we discuss in detail in Chapter Eleven, to be a better fit in your efforts to add an income stream.

11

Network Marketing and Affiliate Programs of Today: "Not Your Father's" Mlm

For those of an entrepreneurial bent, network marketing offers a potentially lucrative, more or less permanent stream of income, built primarily on effort, not capital. The advantages of this type of business allow people to get started with minimal investment, provide a ready product or service to sell, have accounting already in place, and provide marketing and training assistance for the distributor. Most distributors are able to work from their home on their own schedule.

I have been associated with and provided legal services to all manner of network marketing (also known as MLM) companies and their distributors. While many companies who pioneered this industry are well known, such as Avon, Amway, and Mary Kay Cosmetics, there are numerous new ventures offering wine, kitchen wares, lingerie, long distance services, internet services, vitamins and herbal supplements, prepaid legal services, to name a few. It is a highly volatile industry that has survived extremely strong regulatory scrutiny, and even attacks. This scrutiny has been good however in that some of the old "pyramid scheme" type operations are no longer able to operate.

The concept is supposed to work like this:

1. Through regular and loyal use and/or consumption you, yourself become a "product" of whatever flagship product the company for which you become a distributor is promoting.

2. You reach out to your warm market of relatives and close friends to recruit people into your downline organization of distributors to

become a product of the company and to reach out to their relatives and close friends to recruit others who do the same thing.

This is also known as the concept of doubling[1] or duplication which in theory, and many times in practice, results in geometric growth of both product sales and distributors, both for the company and the distributor who got the ball rolling by being a product of the product and reached out to his or her warm market of friends and relatives to recruit them to do the same things, and so on and so on, for many generations of distributors who can trace their lineage to **you**.

It takes hard work, a great product line, a terrific compensation plan, and an energized field of distributors for a new network marketing company to become and remain successful. Once the product sales go flat as they inevitably will in this industry, a minority of companies make serious mistakes in the face of their flat sales, instead of making good decisions which further energize the field of distributors, such as coming out with innovative new products, or changes to the compensation plan which **add** value to the distributors.

The mistakes generally take the form of poor choice of new products being launched and/or **negative** changes to the compensation plan, amounting to arbitrary changes in the compensation plan which are actually a concerted program of "take aways" which are intended to rein in the incomes of the company's key distributors to make up for the company's flat sales or lost profits. The negative changes are all too transparent to the field of distributors as representing attacks on their "income streams," their "residual income" that they have worked so hard to build.

---

1.   One distributor who finds two other distributors within a month, who find two other distributors within a month, who find two others within a month, etc. results in the first distributor in the line having 4096 distributors under him or her by the end of the first year. In other words, 1X 2=2 in Month 1, 2 X 2=4 in Month 2, 4 X 2=8, in Month 3, 8 X 2=16, in Month 4, 16 X 2=32, in Month 5, 32 X 2=64, in Month 6, 64 X 2=128, in Month 7, 128 X 2=256, in Month 8, 256 X 2=512, in Month 9, 512 X 2=1024, in Month 10, 1024 X 2=2048, in Month 11, 2048 X 2=4096 in month 12.

Obviously, this wonderful success on cue rarely works out to this degree of magnitude, mathematical certainty or precision.

Before starting with a new network marketing company or continuing with your existing company, check out the following:

1.   DO make sure the company distributor contract has a one-year buy-back of products guarantee for at least 90 percent of the purchase price.

2.   DO make sure the company actually emphasizes sales to third parties as a part of the company's institutions in place, that it's not just giving lip service to retail sales in its policies and procedures but actually has a track record of retail sales and training practices that emphasize such sales and has reliable and highly verifiable ways of measuring these sales.

3.   DO make sure the company and its distributors are not involved in front loading ("garage qualification") in order to qualify distributors for commissions. Legal network marketing companies require relatively little up front in the way of purchases from their new distributors.

4.   DO make sure the personal monthly maintenance requirement is no more than would be "reasonably" necessary for a distributor and his/her family to comfortably consume each month.

5.   DON'T sign up with a company that makes (or can't or won't keep its distributors from making) earnings representations that are not fully documented and disclosed as median or average earnings for a particular level of attainment within the company's distributor ranks.

6.   DON'T make any earnings representations yourself, and that includes waiving that commission check around. This information is considered inherently unreliable and misleading in that it does not reflect at all on the actual facts of what an average or median earnings figure is for distributors in the company.

HOW DO AFFILIATE PROGRAMS COMPARE TO NETWORK MARKETING?

How They Work

In addition to providing added capabilities to traditional network marketing models, the World Wide Web has brought an innovation on the concept of network marketing itself to the forefront, referred to as Affiliate marketing programs. Companies promoting their products through user/marketers refer to their independent distributors as Affiliates and pay them on a scaled down version of a network marketing compensation plan, usually paying down only one or two levels of Affiliates in a uni-level compensation plan arrangement.

Affiliate programs can be an excellent promotional device for a web based business. The problem with these types of programs for the Affiliate with respect to their income generation capabilities, is that the Affiliate can only build wide (horizontally) and not deep (vertically), thereby severely limiting income potential, just as is the case with most network marketing uni-level compensation plans. This limitation is only partially mitigated by reason of the fact that the web which can be surfed by millions of people per day at what one might consider warp speed, through links from an Affiliate's web site to other websites (e.g., the product or service provider's website), allows a type of horizontal growth of sorts which is comparable to the more vertical geometric growth of the network marketing downlines, through the network marketing concept of "doubling."

Affiliate programs pay the affiliate for referring people to the company's products, or web sites. This may be done through banners or simple word of mouth. Essentially once signed up to be an affiliate, a person makes a commission that can vary between 5%-35% of the purchase price for any product or service to which the affiliate referred someone, followed by that person making a purchase of some item, such as a popular DVD or book. The affiliate becomes the sales person for the manufacturer, retailer or that web site. "Super" affiliates, those with popular high-traffic websites on which a banner for the company with the product or service produces many unique visitors per day, are highly sought after by companies with affiliate programs.

It is easy for anyone to sign up to become an affiliate and easy to add the necessary content to a new affiliate's web site. Software readily available to a payor website also provides the affiliate a "transparent" look into the status of his or her progress in generating customers for the payor website. This is not unlike the recent technological innovations in the network marketing industry's use of the internet to generate sales and the computer software reporting upgrades that allow for real time or nearly real time reporting of all relevant facts of the marketer's success.

There are also affiliate programs that do not require the person clicking through to spend any money and the affiliate still gets paid. Here, the payments are truly pennies per "click through" but if an affiliate has a high traffic site, even those pennies can add up. Search engines have utilized these types of affiliate programs to build usage on their engines. There are user friendly computer programs available for a relatively inexpensive purchase price of as little as a few hundred dollars that will put a person or company in the business of signing up affiliates who post banners on their websites that can be clicked on by visitors who then move on to the payor's website, presumably to make a purchase and generate a commission to the affiliate in the process.

There are a number of good publications should you be interested in further information: Network Marketing Business Journal (708)633-8888 or www.nmbj.com; the book Recruit & Sell by Dr. Keith Laggos; the MLMIA(Multi LevelMarketing International Association at mlmia.com or (949) 833-0570; the Direct Selling Association at dsa.org or (202) 347-8866; Rod Cook at www.mlmwatchdog.com; and the newly formed Distributors Rights Association at www.mlm-dra.com.

12

Marry Wealth!

You are single, divorced, or widowed. You want to have someone to share your life with you.

When we were in our twenties, we usually did not know if the people we were dating were going to be wealthy or even good with handling financial matters, but in our middle years, we are more likely able to make that determination. We certainly don't advocate marrying someone just because they have money, but if you are seeking a mate, why not raise the bar in that search? Make the most of your efforts and spend time meeting people in situations that are more likely to lead to people who are wealthy, or at least who are financially secure.

Meeting someone at a social activity sponsored by your place of worship is perhaps the most traditional way of meeting solid citizens. At the top of our list of opportunities are art museums! Regardless of your career, education, social, or economical background, it would be hard to go to a good art museum and NOT find something there of interest to you. Buy a museum ticket and wander the halls, admire exhibits, enjoy lunch or a snack at the restaurant, and browse through the gift shop. You can spend time there comfortably by yourself or with a friend. Best of all, museums have memberships available and are most welcoming to new people. By becoming a member, you are invited to special events such as previews of new exhibits, social events such as wine tastings, dancing, educational seminars, and fundraising activities. Volunteers are enthusiastically embraced. These are excellent opportunities to meet people, expand one's interests, and help the community.

We listed the art museums first, but the same principles apply to natural history, science and all museums. Pick the one(s) that interest you and get involved.

The symphonies, opera companies, and theatres of course fall into this same category. Don't be inhibited if you don't know anyone or feel that you may not have enough education or money to be part of these groups. Their very existence depends on having a steady flow of members and volunteers to keep all the wheels turning, and these people come from all walks of life.

With the current prices of tickets at major league sporting events resembling what used to be a week's pay, meeting people at sporting events can prove costly, but if sports is a genuine interest of yours, it is a way to "run into" people who can afford to pony up some serious cash to attend.

Are you content with your financial and estate planning knowledge? If you have an interest in increasing your proficiency, take a financial planning course at a local community college or attend some investment seminars. Check your newspapers as there are normally an abundance of seminars, with varying topics. The people you meet on these occasions may not have lots of money, but they will have an interest in financial management which is a step in the right direction.

Are you interested in travel? There are numerous travel clubs, many specializing in singles groups. You will get an idea of a person's financial situation if they are able to travel frequently and luxuriously.

If you are in the workforce, either by choice or desire, you could consider being a travel or tour escort. Cruise lines in particular hire these independent contractors who can be appropriate guides or escorts for cruises. While being a good dancer and having an engaging personality helps, these are legitimate occupations and you must obtain a "CLIA" number and have a working knowledge of history for the areas of your travel. If you are hired by a tour company, you would need an "IATA" number. Obviously, this line of work puts one in direct contact with folks who have the interest and the financial ability to see the world.

Another opportunity through employment is the luxury apartment industry. As a leasing agent, you would be exposed to tenants and potential tenants, many being divorced or widowed and who can afford luxury rents.

Do you like wine? This could be a good way to enjoy the delights of the grape along with the meeting of like minded souls. While many wine distributors sponsor "tastings" for the public, you might prefer to search out smaller wine groups. Get to know some of your local distributors (wine stores) or look in the newspaper for tastings. Attending wine auctions or working wine festivals and fund raisers are other ways of meeting serious wine lovers.

Does cooking interest you? While anyone can do it, a true gourmet spread will usually cost more than an ordinary dinner. One might assume from that that some of the participants are willing to spend more money on food than others. Cooking classes offer many choices, from basic to gourmet, just choose what interests you. A good class offers demonstration, entertainment and often a wine tasting along with the food. The ones we prefer are hands on, where everyone participates rather than just watching the chef but they all can provide a nice social opportunity.

Use the internet, but SMARTLY! There are many singles connections, such as Love.com, that are popular today. There are also specific interest web sites that a person may go to for information and discussions in chat rooms. These can provide opportunities, but you want to be smart and cautious, as some of the people may not be as honest or real as you might believe.

CASE HISTORIES:

Years ago a client of mine, a widow named Elaine, met and eventually married a man she became acquainted with on the internet. She was in her sixties, enthusiastic about learning computer skills, and no fool. They corresponded for three months before meeting in person, and that first meeting was for lunch as a restaurant. She told me that after that much time was spent corresponding, she had indications (by his grammar, spelling, and composition) of his education, principles, interests, and attitudes. She liked what she read, and she even liked him better in the flesh! It is a good match and they are currently enjoying a new life together in Pennsacola, Florida.

Lynn, a paralegal in Phoenix, along with a friend, decided a good place to meet eligible men might be at financial seminars. They did just that and they were right! At one of these functions, Lynn became acquainted with the seminar host, a successful estate attorney and former partner of mine, and eventually married him. Ten years later they have two lovely children and a great life.

Another acquaintance of ours, Mira, emigrated from Poland. She had struggles with perfecting her English, but was able to use that to her advantage as being considered "continental," she was hired at a high-end men's clothing boutique on Rodeo Drive in Los Angeles. There she met a customer who she did eventually marry. These days she gets to be a customer at the boutiques instead of having to work at one.

13

Before You Invest! Plan A

By now, like Lori and John, you should have your lifestyle goal in mind and have an idea of the age at which you would like to retire. You will want to incorporate some of the common sense action plans and consider some of the income generating options that we have discussed in earlier chapters should you need them.

Before you are ready for investment planning to help create and preserve wealth, there are some simple steps to help you get started efficiently:

Step One:

Build a cash reserve equal to at least three months of living expenses that you keep in the bank or in a brokerage money market account. You want these funds to be accessible immediately and to carry no or little risk of loss of principal.

Step Two:

Closely review your insurance. First let's look at your homeowner's policy. You want to make sure the building and contents amounts are up to date. In other words, if your building coverage shows $100,000, could you rebuild your home for that amount? The terrible California fires in 2003 left many homeowners unable to rebuild because they let the amount of coverage lag behind current costs. You should always have the Replacement Cost Endorsement attached to your policy. Use larger deductibles to bring down your annual premiums. While we don't always agree with it, it is a fact that the insurance companies maintain the right to cancel policies due to claims presented or may increase premiums because of claim activity. For these reasons you may be better off paying smaller claims than turning them in to the insurance company. So if you aren't going to turn in a claim for a $200 broken sliding glass door, why not have a $500 deductible and save on the premium?

There are various discounts the insurance companies offer, such as having smoke detectors, alarm systems, carrying your homeowners and auto policies with the same carrier, being non-smokers, good student or driver credits. Another money saver—if you get a moving violation it's usually better to go to traffic class (if offered in your state) and consequently having the ticket removed from your record rather than paying more premium due to it being on your record.

Another way to save money is to have an umbrella policy for liability. For example, you have a $300,000 limit of liability on your homeowner's policy but then purchase an umbrella policy for $1,000,000. It normally is much cheaper to have the total $1,300,000 in coverage by adding the umbrella policy than by having a $1,300,000 policy limit on your homeowner's policy. You can have this same umbrella policy provide additional liability coverage for your automobile policy also, again saving premium dollars.

Your automobile policy should also carry higher deductibles to keep premiums down.

Life Insurance

We are repeatedly asked by clients "how much life insurance do I need" and there is no easy answer. Our philosophy is that while your children are young, the need is greatest as there is the time window of 18 years or so of caring for them. As they mature (you hope they do) and become self-sufficient (you really hope they do!) the need for life insurance lessens. As one nears retirement, having enough insurance to cover one's liabilities such as home mortgages, credit card debt, auto loans and burial expenses may be sufficient. There certainly are exceptions to this, such as a spouse having extensive medical needs, using life insurance trusts for estate planning, the type of policy carried and its corresponding cost. A term policy for example might be reasonably priced now but will increase substantially at age 60 when it renews. On the other hand, you may have a great universal life policy that is increasing cash value to your satisfaction so keeping it, or perhaps just decreasing the face value to cover your current needs, may be the way to go.

Let's discuss the different types of life insurance so you can make the best choice for your individual situation.

Term Insurance

Keeping it simple, a term insurance policy is like renting coverage. You pay the premium and the insurance company promises to pay your beneficiary a death benefit upon your demise. There is no build up of cash values in these policies. Usually this is the least expensive way to obtain life insurance while you are middle-aged. You can buy a policy that has an increase annually in the premium or you could choose one that has the same premium for a ten or twenty year period, with the premium increasing at the end of the period. This is good cheap insurance that provides coverage for most circumstances, but, upon turning 60 or 65, most policies have huge premium increases. When we say huge, we mean huge. If you are going to need a substantial amount of coverage in your later years due to a much younger spouse, a special needs child, or high debt, this might not be the most efficient way to go. In such instances, a combination of term and permanent coverage may work better for your cash flow.

You may be buying group term insurance at your place of employment. Again, this is a very inexpensive way to obtain insurance but the problem is that when you leave the company, you also leave your coverage. You will be older, and therefore buying a new policy will cost more or you may have a medical situation which prohibits your even qualifying for an individual policy. We normally recommend you use the company group policy to supplement your insurance needs but that you obtain your own policy as a basic tenet of your financial planning.

Surprisingly, term insurance is one of the few things that is cheaper now than in the past. The reason for this is that people are living longer which means they pay life insurance premiums for a longer period of time and the insurance companies have a longer time before having to pay beneficiaries. We strongly recommend that you check the rates for a new term policy against what you are currently paying on an older policy. And we also recommend you check who you have listed as beneficiaries on your old policies. Unlikely as it seems, people do forget to change these as their life changes. You may have a different spouse, more children, or may still be reflecting your mother as you weren't married when you originally took out the policy. We have seen it all and some situations are very sad, but these beneficiary designations take precedence over wills or trusts. He who is designated reaps the benefits!

Permanent Insurance

Permanent insurance is designed to provide death benefits, the same as term insurance, but also the opportunity to build up cash value in the policy. This opportunity of course means the premiums are more costly than term. There are three main types of policies, Whole Life, Universal Life, and Variable Universal Life.

Whole Life

Whole Life insurance is designed to having the insurance company invest some of the premium, thereby giving the policy owner a little extra cash value along with the death benefits. The return is quite small—a two percent return on your money would be not be uncommon. For that reason, whole life is not currently a very popular concept.

Universal Life

Building on the whole life (cash value) theme, insurance companies later designed a policy that invested some of the premium more aggressively, so that policyholders would be encouraged by a potentially larger cash value build up. These can work if the insurance company has invested wisely. From our perspective, universal life has a slightly higher premium than whole life, but can be a good option when someone is looking for a policy to keep for a lifetime. Universal life is often the vehicle of choice when insurance is used in some estate planning techniques, such as an ILIT, Irrevocable Life Insurance Trust.

Words of Caution

You may expect to be pretty much debt free and/or to have a sizeable investment portfolio by retirement and are therefore comfortable using term insurance to cover your current needs. If so, work hard toward those goals as we have counseled a number of people who face the dilemma of how to pay for the large premiums after reaching age 65 because they still have substantial liabilities that they want covered in case of their death. Again, it really depends on your individual circumstances but having a small permanent policy that you keep and a term policy that goes away after the bulk of your protection needs decrease might work well.

Another area of concern when dealing with life insurance is that you could have an old policy(ies) that has cash value and an agent may want to rollover or exchange that into a new policy. Sometimes this can be a good thing to accomplish your goals but sometimes not. You will want to deal with an advisor whom you trust. Also bear in mind that if you do an exchange within the first four or five years of your old policy's beginning date, you will undoubtedly lose most if not all of your cash value. A policy that has been around for about ten years or more usually is a better candidate for an exchange.

BE SURE you have your new policy positively guaranteed before surrendering your old one as you might be uninsurable now. Always check the rating of the insurance company and we recommend staying with those A or better. Go to insure.com to get these ratings online or ask your agent.

If you have a health problem, don't give up if you need insurance. There are companies that we call "health problem friendly". In other words, they specialize in impaired risks—say people who have had cancer or who currently have some type of heart disease. Some names you might want to check out: Manhattan Life Insurance, Connecticut National and U.S. Financial.

Disability Insurance

Disability insurance, which is very important during your earning years, has less impact as you near retirement. Most policies will provide coverage only until a person reaches age 65 so you need to consider the premium you are paying against potential benefits which will cease when you reach 65.

Medical Insurance

Medical insurance, as we covered in an earlier chapter, is paramount until you and your spouse reach 65. If you plan on retiring before age 65, you will want to make sure you either can continue on with your present employer's group policy until reaching 65 or that you have an individual policy. Individual policies are much more expensive than if you are on a group plan and even more importantly, you want to be sure you both qualify for a policy. Just because you were covered under your employer's policy does not mean you can qualify for an individual policy. It is critical to check it out before making a move.

Step Three:

Meet with an estate attorney to obtain a Revocable Living Trust. There are very few exceptions to this rule. A Revocable Living Trust bypasses probate, which is a timely and expensive and public way to handle one's estate. Most Revocable Living Trusts have the spouses as trustees during their lifetime, who lose no control over their assets and potentially save on a variety of taxes. The Trust also provides Medical Powers of Attorney, Durable Powers of Attorney (in case of incompetence by one of the spouses) and specifies the desires of the spouses (or individuals) on how they want their legacy handled. Specific issues, such as children from previous marriages, adult children with special needs, gifting and so forth are all handily worked out in the Trust. These trusts are called Revocable because they can be changed at the will of the trustees. Costs will vary but most estate attorneys charge fees of $1,000 to $3,500 for a standard trust. We do recommend that you use an experienced estate attorney for your trusts. We have seen some regrettable situations where people have hoped to save on costs and used paralegal type services or attorneys not specifically experienced in estate matters where the family ultimately had avoidable financial losses because of the quality of the trusts or incompetence.

Frequently Asked Questions About Trusts:

If I have a will, why do I need a trust?

A will does not avoid Probate. In fact, it is a one way ticket to Probate Court as when you die, all wills must be verified by the Probate Court. A will does not provide protection if you become incompetent—a real concern for many older Americans. You could easily find yourself in a conservatorship, under the control of the Probate Court before you pass away.

What is Probate?

Probate is the legal procedure whereby the court makes sure that when you die, your debts are paid and your estate is distributed according to your will.

What is so bad about Probate?

Probate is expensive. Your debts, attorney and executor fees and other costs must be paid before anything can be passed to your heirs.

Probate takes time. The average probate takes 18 months and while your estate is being probated, the assets are usually frozen. If your loved ones need money to live on, they will have to ask the court for funds.

Your family has no privacy as all Probate files are public records.

Doesn't Joint Tenancy avoid Probate?

> It just postpones it to the death of the second spouse, when the assets are probated before distribution to your heirs.

Is Transferring Property into the Trust difficult?

> No and the trust paperwork will include letters to banks, stockbrokers and so forth to explain how to title your assets.

Do I Lose Control of the Assets in My Trust?

> No! You remain in complete control of all property in your trust. As the trustee and trustor of your trust, you can buy, sell, borrow, lend and spend any way you choose. You can amend or cancel the trust at any time also.

What is a Successor Trustee and What Does He (She) Do?

> Generally each spouse is a Trustee; when the second of the spouses pass on, the Successor Trustee steps in to manage the trust according to the instructions you have previously set up. He will pay your bills, do whatever is necessary to keep your financial affairs in order, and make sure your assets are distributed according to your wishes. Successor Trustees are typically your adult children, other relatives, or trusted friends.

Marital, Bypass and QTIP (Qualified Terminal Remainder Trusts)

These are normally included in and as part of your Revocable Living Trust, if they are appropriate for accomplishing your estate planning goals. The QTIP is particularly effective when there are children from a previous marriage to be provided for while providing also for the current family.

ILIT (Irrevocable Life Insurance Trust)

Used in estate planning to save on federal estate taxes, normally for people who have estates over the federal exemption amount, which is $1,500,000 per person in 2004. These are irrevocable, meaning once you have established one, it is cast in concrete!

Charitable Remainder Trusts (CRT)

The typical profile of a user of a CRT is one (or a couple) who have highly appreciated assets that they want to eliminate payment of the capital gains, they want to donate to a charity, they will obtain a sizable immediate tax advantage, and they will collect income from the proceeds until they die. Whatever remains of the proceeds from the asset at the time of the second spouse's death is what is then transferred to the charity. These are gaining popularity particularly with people who own investment property that has exploded in market value. Sometimes an ILIT is used in conjunction with the CRT to benefit heirs that otherwise would have lost out on an inheritance of the asset.

Step Four:

Have a formal financial plan completed by a Certified Financial Planner™ for you. This will be a road map for both you and your investment counselor to determine how much money you will need and when you will need it. A good planner will assist you to establish your risk tolerance, will incorporate tax strategies, will implement the plan, monitor the plan, revise the plan when needed, and rebalance your portfolio on a timely basis. Fees will vary, and usually there is just one original charge regardless of future changes incorporated into the plans for clients. A reasonable range will be from $500 to $3,500 plus, depending on the complexity.

So what really is financial planning? Simply put, it is meeting your life goals through proper management of your finances. For most of us, day to day concerns are distracting, preventing us from thinking about our financial futures. Or we may simply feel overwhelmed and not know where to start. Even the do-it-yourselfers of investing will gain peace of mind by having a plan in place. Checking that plan annually to determine if you are on schedule for where you need to be is paramount to reaching your goals. Some wise person once said "even the longest journey begins with a single step".

As you can see, financial planning is an ongoing process, requiring adaptation as your needs evolve and the market conditions change. Because of that, you will want to have a financial planner with whom you are totally comfortable as well as having confidence in his/her abilities. While there are a number of designations in the field of financial planning, we highly recommend the CFP®, or Certified Financial Planner™. To qualify for the designation, they must have fulfilled a rigorous study regimen which usually takes a three year period to complete. You can contact the Financial Planning Association, website www.fpanet.org for information regarding CFPs® in your area, their specific practice parameters, their specialties and so on.

We do realize that not everyone will or can do these last two steps, at least at the beginning of their savings plan. Don't be discouraged, regardless of your circumstances. The important thing is that you begin now. Relax and read the next chapter for Plan B.

14

Relax and Check out Plan B

You're feeling anxious about your retirement. You haven't begun saving or have very little savings accumulated so far. You don't have the cash flow to see the estate attorney for a revocable living trust or an investment advisor for a financial plan right now. You are humbled by what you feel is a lack of dedication or discipline on your part to have an adequate retirement savings pot. David and I have met many people in that frame of mind, who have said they were embarrassed to seek out professional assistance because of it. Stop! Know you can indeed "Sprint to the Finish" in different ways. That was our motivation to write this book in the first place.

There are simple systems for getting on track that require no detailed calculations of future lifestyle need, no budgeting, no hand wringing and you can learn them by reading this book in the comfort and privacy of your own home.

Numbers are Not Everything!

First, ignore those big numbers that you see in investment articles in the newspapers and magazines. I have read so much planner advice that is based on retirement calculations that spit out huge numbers, such as needing a million dollars to realize such and such. That number may or may not be representative of what someone is trying to accomplish, but to most people, a million dollar figure can be discouraging and make one want to give up before even starting. There are by the way, 293 million Americans and 280 million of those are not millionaires!

Get in the Game

While you can't control the future the present is in your hands. You are going to start by paying yourself first. You need to get in the habit of saving so your money can start working for you. While any savings, however modest, will help, we would recommend you strive to put 5% of every paycheck away. As you are able, try to increase that amount to 10% of every paycheck.

It makes the most sense to begin with putting that savings into a tax deferred retirement account, which we will call Bucket Number 1. These retirement plans can be a company sponsored 401-k or 457, but if those are not available to you, the next best option is a traditional IRA or a Roth IRA. If you are self-employed, you could be eligible to open your own retirement plan, such as a SEP-IRA, a Simple IRA, or an individual 401-k. Because most of these plans offer benefits other than just saving, they should be your first choice. We will discuss these various plans in detail later, but for now understand they are simple to participate in or set up.

If you work for a company that has a 401-k plan, the forms to join up should be readily available. If you are self-employed, the options mentioned above can be established at a brokerage house, directly with a mutual fund company, or a bank, to name a few. Years ago some retirement plans were complicated and costly to setup, but competition has changed that.

Ideally you will maximize the savings allowed in your retirement plan, which we will call Bucket Number One. Now, to save more you will open a regular investment program, which we will call Bucket Number Two and you are going to DO IT THE EASY WAY. In other words, set up an automatic program with a brokerage, bank or mutual fund company. All you have to do is make a call to get the forms, sign and return them along with a voided check and money will automatically be debited from your bank account every month and deposited into your investment savings account. This is great for several reasons—you don't have to do anything once it is set up; you won't spend the money because you don't have access to it as it is automatically saved; it allows you to invest with much less money than if you started with a lump sum as most investments have minimums; you end up Dollar Cost Averaging as when you buy investment shares every month, you wind up buying more shares when the price is low and buying less when the price goes up. Overall you end up with more shares. This dollar cost averaging technique can be used on your retirement plans also.

Remember that to decrease anxiety when contemplating retirement, think of monthly cash flow needs instead of the big number of assets needed. Let's continue to focus on ways to decrease monthly outgo and/or increase monthly income.

Your Residence Provides Options

Your home can be a major factor. Ideally you would want to have the house paid off when you take retirement. But that situation will not apply to everyone. You may sell your home and rent or buy something less expensive, like the couple Lori and John are doing. Any left over amounts of equity then become part of your nest egg. If you must retire and still have a sizable mortgage, check out the following refinance options.

For some retirees, it is a fact of life that they will be making house payments until they are in their 80s, and if that is the case, lowering their monthly payment may be the best solution for their cash flow. This can be accomplished in several different ways. If you have an 8.5% fixed rate mortgage, you will reduce your payment if you can refinance to a 6% fixed rate mortgage.

But what if you already have a 6% rate for a 30 year fixed mortgage and the new loans are about those same rates? Let's say you have been paying on your loan for 10 years. You can still reduce monthly payments by taking out a new loan because although the interest rate might remain the same, you are spreading out over a new 30 year term a smaller loan amount as you have paid down principal in those past 10 years. This technique is not optimal as it decreases future equity, but again if it could give you a better current quality of life which may be your priority.

This leads us directly to another option connected with home ownership. It is called the Reverse Mortgage. A relatively new concept in the past few years, these loans are slowly becoming mainstream.

A reverse mortgage is a loan that provides the borrower with tax free money that can be received in a lump sum, a monthly payment or a line of credit as long at the person resides in their home. A borrower must be at least 62 years of age and either own their home outright or have a very low mortgage balance that can be paid off at the loan closing. The loan requires no repayment until the borrower either sells their home or becomes deceased and it passes into their estate. When it does pass into the estate, heirs can never owe more than the value of the home.

These loans are not for everyone. Obviously they use the equity of the home so there is less, if any, legacy to pass on to heirs. As with newer innovations, people need to research to make sure the company providing the loan is trustworthy and not over charging with loan origination points and costs. We are seeing the larger banks and some brokerage houses enter this field. They are the logical places for retirees to seek assistance and have the confidence that they are dealing with a credible lender. And these loans can provide great comfort for homeowners who prefer to remain in their home for their final years who might otherwise not be able to do so.

Contact Fannie Mae (800) 732-6643 or www.fanniemae.com and request "Home Keeper: It Pays to Keep You in Your Home. Also there is the National Center for Home Equity Conversion at www.reverse.org or HUD (800) 569-4287 or www.hudhcc.org.

Don't Make Loans to Uncle Sam!

The tax reform bill that recently passed reduced the federal tax rates. What does that mean to you right now? That if you are working, the amount of tax withheld from your paychecks is probably more than what you are going to owe when you send in your tax return next April. Decrease your withholdings (it's a simple form you fill out for your employer) and put that extra money into savings! There is no good reason to pay Uncle Sam early and wait for a return when you could have your money out there working for you in an investment savings account.

Health Savings Accounts

Another new tax favored option for you to consider is the Health Savings Account (HSA). Almost anyone under age 65 can have a HSA who buys a high deductible health insurance policy and is not covered by other health insurance. Your policy must have at least a $1,000 deductible for individuals or $2,000 for families. You can contribute whatever your deductible amount is up to $2,600 for singles or $5,150 for families. The tax breaks for you are as follows: you can deduct the HSA contributions and the account can grow tax deferred, just like an IRA. Withdrawals are tax-free at any time you use the money to pay qualified medical expenses. There are no income limitations for an HSA. You can spend the HSA money on doctor and dental care, hospital costs, prescription and non-prescription drugs, vision, and qualified long term care insurance premiums. The money you don't use continues to grow in the HAS for use in later years. There is no "use it or lose it rule". There is a 10% penalty plus a tax bill if you use the HSA money for non medical expenses before age 65. You'll pay taxes but no penalty for non-medical withdrawals after that.

You can open an HSA with some insurance companies—Assurant, Golden Rule, and several Blue Cross/Blue Shield plans. More insurance companies are expected to follow suit soon. If you work for someone, check with your employer to see if the HSA is available for you. If you are self-employed, check with your insurance carrier or eHealthInsurance.com for insurance companies who offer an HSA.

These HSAs have a benefit not shown above—in order to use them you need to have a high deductible on your medical insurance policy. That high deductible will reduce your premium cost if you previously had a lower deductible.

To Mix or Not to Mix!

While you will hear "diversify, diversify" from investment counselors, ourselves included, you can get started with a minimal number of investments. Mutual funds are a natural choice for most beginning investors for several reasons. You do not have to spend time trying to analyze which stocks you should buy, hold or sell—the fund manager will do that for you. The majority of funds hold an average of 50 stocks. Were you to buy 50 individual stocks yourself with limited funds, you would incur unrealistic transaction costs relative to your investment. You will have to decide, of course, what funds to buy and it can be as simple as 60% stock funds and 40% bond funds. In general, we invest in stocks to provide growth and buy bonds to add stability and income to the portfolio. As you get nearer retirement, the bond percentage is often increased. We have detailed investment recommendations later in the book but you can do this simply.

Even simple strategy requires periodic maintenance. We encourage you to check your portfolio with the idea of rebalancing at least once a year. What do we mean by rebalancing? Let's say you are investing 50% into bond funds and 50% into stock funds but at year end, the stock market went down so your market valuations now reflect 70% bonds and 30% stocks. Sell 20% of the bonds and buy 20% more of stocks to get your portfolio back "in balance." Not only does this keep you on track for your goals, but it forces you to sell high and buy low, which is the optimum in investing.

15

Pitfalls of Retirement Planning

We have spent many chapters discussing what to do for retirement planning but little about what not to do. Let's explore the pitfalls so you will know what to avoid.

Simple as it sounds, not thinking about your retirement can have dire consequences. People who do not have some plan for how to live those retirement years, which may well extend over a 30 or 40 year period, will have more anxiety and less fun, the psychologists tell us. We believe them! As the wife of one recently retired couple said, "I took him in sickness and in health, for better or for worse, but I didn't think that included all breakfasts, lunches, and dinners". It is not uncommon for new retirees to become depressed, feeling less self worth due to a lack of purpose. Without outside interests and activity, it is easy to become self absorbed with one's aging process, and the accompanying aches and pains and boredom. When you are visualizing your retirement, think about what interests you, what you wish to accomplish, what changes will you have to deal with, what fears you might have, what opportunities might be presented to you? By tackling some of these issues head on, you will have more energy and confidence to make your retirement dreams come true. This is the time of your life to be proactive and seek satisfaction. After all, you have worked long and hard to reach retirement status.

Not Thinking

Neglecting your finances is another minefield! Call it a lack of attention. We know people are very busy and thinking about money matters can easily take a backseat to life's daily challenges. Successful wealth creation takes a commitment of time. If you can't make that commitment, hire someone you trust to get you on track.

Financial Windfalls

Next is mismanaging financial windfalls. These windfalls come in different guises—inheritance, lottery winnings, stock options, and severance packages and they each have their own peculiarities.

Research shows over half of lottery winners are broke within a few years of winning. I personally have counseled several winners at the time of their winning. Receiving a tremendous amount of money is a traumatic experience that can override the joy of having no financial burdens. The stress of having to make lots of decisions, many with emotional impact, takes a toll. All of the winners immediately changed their telephone numbers and most moved from their homes soon afterwards as they were deluged (relentlessly) by family, friends, co-workers, charities, and total strangers for gifts, loans, contributions and investment opportunities. None of the winners I worked with were financially knowledgeable so deciding which attorney, financial planner and CPA to consult with created anxiety. Who were they to trust? What advice were they to heed? Even deciding whether to immediately quit their job, what kind of car to buy (interestingly each one did buy a new car right away!) or should they move, were debilitating issues when thrown at them so quickly. We recommend not making any major decisions for a few months when the dust has had time to settle. One practical piece of advice—take a 30 day world cruise and leave your cell phone at home. You become inaccessible and it gives you the space to and opportunity to think, make plans, and yes, even celebrate your good fortune at your own pace.

Inheriting can provide two distinct situations. If the inheritance is a surprise, managing it is stressful for many of the same reasons mentioned above. A private inheritance may afford you more privacy than standing in front of a TV camera with a million dollar check but the many decisions attached to it have a price.

If an inheritance is expected, many of us in the financial and estate planning businesses will concur it can have an adverse effect on the beneficiaries. Their motivation to succeed in life on their own merits can be weakened if they visualize that inheritance carrot always in front of themselves. And there is always the risk that for some, grandpa at age 83 marries a 65 year old sweetie who will make sure grandpa's money is spent before it trickles down to expectant relatives.

More prevalent is that the amount anticipated by the heirs is more than they ultimately receive. There are estate taxes, income taxes, capital gains taxes, market and real estate valuation risks, probate or legal costs that can deplete the coffers. We caution our clients that unless they are intimately involved with the estate and tax situation of the donor to plan conservatively for their expected legacy.

A third inheritance, in a broad context, is the result of the death of a spouse. The impact of dealing with the emotions can be overwhelming. There are certain things that will require early attention, such as notifying Social Security, any pension companies, life insurance companies, annuity companies and your banks. You will need to order certified death certificates in order to deal with the above, and you will need to have a final estate tax return completed within nine months of the death. Yes, you also need to advise your broker/dealer but you should put off making any changes in your investments until you have had time to get comfortable with your new circumstances.

Severance Packages

Severance packages can lessen the blow of unplanned unemployment, but one wants to be careful not to rest on one's laurels if a steady job is still a necessity. The emotional impact of being laid off might lure a person into using that money to do some "feel good" things. Try to save that bonus and hit the job search as quickly as possible. The longer you stop the rhythm of steady work, the more difficult job searching becomes. That severance pay would be a welcome addition to your eventual retirement pot so don't use it indiscriminately.

Stock Options

Stock Options have their own special sets of rules. You will need to understand what type of tax you may trigger upon exercising and then selling your shares. It could be income tax or capital gains tax or the dreaded alternative minimum tax or all of them! There may be sale restrictions, timing limitations and stock market risk to be dealt with prior to getting the cash in hand. Other conditions, such as if the options are in a tax deferred plan can have far reaching implications based on how you handle them. You will have two choices. One is to roll the shares over into a regular IRA; the other is to take out the shares and pay the taxes due on the basis of the shares. We strongly recommend you confer with a CPA who is well versed in stock options before taking any action.

Unprotected Assets

Let's talk about leaving assets unprotected. One of the greatest wealth destroyers is the cost of medical care as we age. A study done by the New England Journal of Medicine states that 43% of people age 65 are expected to enter a nursing home at least once before they die. Many people are in denial as we surely don't want to think about that for ourselves. If you haven't had a relative or family friend who has gone through this process you may not have given it much thought at all. For those who have experienced it, you know the mental and financial strain it can bring to the entire family. You need to become aware of Long Term Care Insurance. Not everyone needs it. The very rich basically self-insure and the very poor can't afford it. For all the rest of us in the middle, it's worth taking a look at.

Myths vs.Reality. Medicare/Medicaid or health insurance will pay for long term care costs. Not true. When discussing this issue it is important to know the difference between "skilled care" and "custodial care".

Skilled care connotes intensive nursing and rehabilitative care under direct supervision by a nurse and the general direction of a physician. Custodial care on the other hand does not require medical training. It is primarily care that is needed to assist a person in what is called the activities of daily living, such as meal preparation, personal hygiene, dressing and undressing, transferring out of bed, and administering routine medicine.

Medicare pays for skilled care only. While long term care is generally considered custodial care, even the skilled care that is covered under most circumstances by Medicare has a maximum of 100 days of coverage only. Medicaid, a Federal/State welfare program is designed to aid the poor who have basically no assets. Medicaid benefits are treated as a lien and become the responsibility of the family. In other words, Medicaid collects the "loan" from the estate of the family members after the care recipient's death. Medicaid planning where there is a desire to legally exempt certain assets from the Medicaid lien's reach is difficult at best and requires the skills of an experienced elder law attorney.

According to a MetLife Mature Market Institute study of August 2003, the national average nursing home cost is $181 per day, more than $5,000 a month and is rising at nearly four times the rate of inflation. Combine those figures with the fact that often one spouse still resides in the family residence, still has his or her living costs to deal with and the total monthly figure will quickly deplete the retirement nest egg.

Long term care insurance is specifically designed to help pay for room, board, and custodial costs. Because your acceptability to obtain this insurance and the premiums are subject to your health and your age, we recommend that people check out policies ideally from age 45 through 59. There are a number of factors that also affect the premiums, such as a the deductible/elimination amount (choose a 90 day elimination period to decrease premiums), the length of coverage during which benefits will be paid (such as a three year policy or a lifetime policy term), the amount of the daily benefit (typically $100 or $200 per day and we strongly recommend adding an inflation rider), and the level of the comprehensive nature of the coverage (we urge you to consider coverage which includes home health care as well as nursing home care).

A waiver of premium is a good thing as it means your premium payments will stop after you have been receiving benefits for a period of time, usually 90 days. Often insurance companies will give a spousal discount for married couples who apply and are issued coverage at the same time. Make sure the insurance company is financially sound and you can research using several rating organizations such as A.M.Best, Standard & Poor's, Moody's and Duff & Phelps. We personally recommend a rating minimum of "A-." One last thought on Long Term Care Insurance, you usually do not buy it to have all your costs covered; it is a tool to help keep those costs be manageable.

Cash Flow

Another pitfall is not managing your cash flow. You have to remember that once you retire, especially if it is with a limited nest egg, you must spend less than you have coming in. It may mean a change of habits in your shopping, dining out, and gift giving. Some splurges are worth it, and eating more hamburger and beans to make up for them occasionally is okay. Being aware of your income/outgo will keep you out of trouble.

Studies, such as "Consumption in Retirement: Survey Evidence on Expectations and Outcomes" by John Ameriks of the TIAA-CREF Institute, Caplin, and John Leahy of Boston University, documents the uncertainty that pre-retirees have about expenses in retirement and the fact that quite a number of people end up being surprised at how expensive things are in retirement.

As noted, retirees reported that the actual retirement spending declined less than expected, the difference averaging about 8 or 9 percentage points. For example, those expecting to reduce spending about 15% in retirement only experienced a 6% reduction.

Tax Planning

Another aspect of managing your cash is tax planning. David and I have seen many examples of couples who wanted to save money by doing their own tax returns but lost big time as they missed some good tax savings. I know everyone will not agree with me on this point, but the IRS regs are thousands of pages long and even the CPAs, who do this for a living, have to work to stay current on all the issues.

If you are turning 70 ½, you must begin taking what the IRS calls your Required Minimum Distribution from your IRAs, retirement plans such as 401-ks, Profit Sharing and so on. Even if you are so fortunate that you don't need the money to live on, IRS is waiting in the bushes to collect the taxes that are due on it and should you neglect this process, the penalty is a 50% of what you should have taken as well as the ordinary income taxes due. It is pretty simple as the government has published rate tables that tell you the percentage you need to take each year. Any custodian (that is where your IRA or retirement plan is kept, such as a brokerage, bank, insurance or mutual fund company) can assist you with getting this on track.

The only IRA exempt from this Required Minimum Distribution rule is a Roth-IRA.

If you are no longer working you won't have taxes withheld from a paycheck. Since Uncle Sam wants his tax money right away, you will now have two choices about how to pay them. You can either make estimated quarterly payments, based on what you expect to have due on your next tax return, or you can have taxes withheld from your Social Security or pension. Most people prefer the first option, but whatever your choice, do it immediately as if you don't you will be hit with a penalty when you file your annual return.

Know Thyself!

Another pitfall: Not Knowing Thyself! When you either chose your own investments or worked with your financial planner to design a portfolio, your risk tolerance should have been a incremental part of that design. What we mean is that even if technology stocks or mutual funds were flying high at the time, those choices had to be considered risky. Did you consequently suffer anxiety when the market plummeted? If you are like most of us, of course you did. When we are in a booming marketplace, it is easy to forget about how much we can stand to lose but history tells us the market is cyclical and our investments should have some defenses built in to withstand the downward slides. Remember financial planning is really life planning—it is fluid and circumstances will change that require action on your part. In most cases the best way to manage risk is to apply two fundamental investment principles: a long term perspective and diversification of your investments.

Not All Trusts are to be Trusted

David discussed the merits of Revocable Living Trusts in an earlier chapter. Don't confuse those with this next subject—foreign trusts or off-shore trusts. We continue to marvel at how people can still be fooled by a promise to eliminate taxes or hide assets from creditors or even divorcing spouses by using the foreign or off-shore trusts.

First of all there are legitimate trusts and if properly structured and administered, some people in high risk professions, such at GYN/OB's, have been known to execute them. A properly done foreign trust is very expensive and has many strings attached to them. And these trusts never eliminate taxes. You will notice on the front of your federal tax return there is a box on the first page to check off if you have a foreign trust. We call it the "please audit me IRS" for they surely will do so!

For the majority of folks, these trusts do not make sense. If you happen to be in a profession at high risk for litigation, such as medicine, you may still wish for protection against creditors. There is an alternative as several states have created legal loopholes allowing Domestic Asset Protection Trusts. Delaware, Alaska, Nevada, Rhode Island and Utah have enacted laws legalizing a self-settled trust offering some asset protection from creditors. But beware, the courts are still debating the legality of these trusts and you will want to obtain counsel from lawyers who are well versed in this area before jumping in.

To Deed or Not to Deed

As retirees as they find themselves needing more assistance as they grow older, a common question is asked of us. Should we put our adult child on the deed to our home? No, no, no! Adding that son's name on the deed while you are alive will accomplish a number of things, most with negative impacts.

He now owns half your home. Yes, once you pass on it eliminates going through Probate Court to put the home entirely in his name, but he also has lost the step up in cost basis. What does that mean? Well, depending on how the deed is titled, he will have some taxes to pay on the amount between your cost basis and selling price. If the house is passed on after death, his cost basis would be the market value as of the date of your death. If he sold the property immediately for that price, he would not have to pay any capital gains taxes. If he is on the deed at your death, the tax man calleth. If you have tons of equity, that could be a big number. Long term gains are currently taxed at 15% for the feds but remember you will also have to pay your state taxes, which in California, for example, would be another 9.3%.

Now lets go back to "he now owns half your home." You lose sole control over things like selling your home, refinancing your home, doing a reverse mortgage loan, getting a home equity loan. In theory, he is responsible for half the property taxes and half the mortgage, if any, and he is entitled to half the tax deductions. If his assets become subject to any liens due to a lawsuit or even a divorce, you could lose your home in the deal.

There are a few exceptions to this rule, some used in advanced estate strategy, but these will not apply to vast the majority of retirees.

Tapping a Retirement Plan

If you are still employed and under 59 ½, do not borrow from your retirement plan. Don't even think about it! Don't let it enter your thought processes. Pretend you don't have it!

Today most workers with 401-k or 403-b retirement plans can borrow from them. Typically the plans allow a loan of up to half your vested amount, subject to a $50,000 maximum. Some plans may further restrict borrowing for specific reasons, like a home purchase, education or medical expenses. You usually have to repay the loan within a five year period and you do have to pay yourself interest too.

While it can be enticing to think about funding a pool for the home or a new car, remember if you don't repay the loan you will have to pay federal and state income tax on the amount and if you are under age 59 ½, you will also pay a 10% early withdrawal penalty. For many that means you would realistically get about 50% as a net spend able amount from what you borrowed. Even if you mean to pay the loan back, if you leave your employer for any reason, the loan is due in full or it will be considered an early distribution and all the taxes will be due. That could move you into a higher tax bracket that year, to add to your woes.

But just as importantly, you are giving up tax free compounding earnings on the money you withdraw which could lead to a significantly smaller nest egg come retirement.

Get Rich Short Cuts

Will get you into trouble! Your chances of quick ways to invest to make up a nest egg usually are bad choices.

Home Equity for Stock Purchase

How often David and I have heard the question—"why not use our home equity to invest? Our loan rate is lower than the return we can make in the market?" First of all most home equity lines are variable, meaning they will move as the interest rates in the market place move. Even if you were getting a better return on an investment today, it might be less than your home equity loan rate next month. That investment can lose value any day in the marketplace. You are playing roulette with losing home equity and adding current debt to your situation. It is not a good way to enter your retirement!

Hey, the Market is Up and I Want a Margin Account!

When you use a margin account, it means you are borrowing money from your broker to buy stock that you don't have the cash to pay for. Brokerage firms are usually happy to accommodate their clients with providing margin accounts because their business is to buy and sell investments. The more trades that are done the more revenue the brokerage firm makes.

This may seem fine until the investments you purchased on margin have decreased in value and the brokerage firm gives you a margin call. Typically you will have a period of time, say 72 hours, to pay off the margin debt in your account. If you can't come up with the cash, they will sell enough of your portfolio to cover the debt. Consider that margin calls are most frequent when the market is down, meaning that it might be a bad time to have to sell investments to cover the call. This can be a risky and costly strategy.

I'm Going to Day Trade!

I am going to save money by doing my own trading on the internet. I have access to all the research I need on the internet. I can do it!

You most likely will not be able to do it! Professional institutional buyers, stock brokers and mutual fund managers consider that they are doing well if they make the right choices 70% of the time and they have teams that provide research and analysis to give them guidance. Day trading encompasses even more obstacles than the professionals face, such as paying commissions on small trades, which cut dramatically into your profits. Taxes will be another factor that whittle away at potential profit as to qualify for capital gains tax rates, you must hold the investment for one year before selling. With day trading, the quick buy/sells will be taxed at ordinary income tax rates.

Getting From Point A to Point B

You need a plan to efficiently get from here to retirement. We have said before, but it is so important it begs repeating that you need to see what you desire. Sit in a comfortable chair and imagine yourself a year or two from now. Visualize what clothes you are wearing, what activities you are engaged in and the location you are in. Be clear and be specific. It's hard and might take some practice but that just reinforces the goal.

One reason people fail to reach their goals is that those goals were never clear to begin with.

Psychologists tell us that once you have your vision, focus on how you are feeling about it. Many times what you think you want doesn't really make you as happy as you thought it would.

Write the Goal Down

You have heard this before but it is so true. I am and have been "a goal writer down person" for twenty years. By writing them down you can refer to them more often and reinforce your will to execute them. If you need to change the goal, cross it off and write down the new one. Writing them down also helps you to not forget them. When you see something you hold the image for about a half-second. When you hear something, you retain it somewhat longer. You can easily lose it unless there is a conscious effort to retain it.

The Action Plan

Break each goal into pieces you can realistically achieve. You may want to contribute the maximum $13,000 to your 401-k this year and it is easier to contribute the $1,083 per month than coming up with the whole thing in December.

Be a good goal setter and you will get pay-offs. Working towards your goals will give you even greater pay-offs. Research shows those who steadily work towards their goals, and even achieve them as they go along, are overall very happy with their lives. People just starting to work on goals even report feeling more useful and content.

However, you can't just think about goals without some action to get the ball rolling. Go on automatic to make life easier on yourself. Go directly to that class or gym after work rather than going home first; sign up for automated payments from your paycheck directly into your 401-k plan. The less chances you have to thwart yourself the more chances you will have to succeed.

Remove Barriers!

There are going to be obstacles in your way and they need to be dealt with. Your spouse or a good friend might be threatened if you lose weight; your adult child can't understand why you won't help him with a financial problem; you know buying new shoes comforts you in times of stress; you may be inherently afraid of the success you want.

Recognize the barriers. Some will be more difficult to deal with but others can be managed more easily, such as avoiding your favorite shoe shop! Surround yourself with people who give you positive feedback.

The Habit Tune-Up

If you are making changes to help you get to your goals, there will be some old habits that will have to be replaced with new ones. If you are used to popcorn, drinks, and candy at the movies, try having dinner right before you go. You will save money and calories. Skip going out to dinner just one night a month and add that $70 dollar savings to your regular monthly mortgage payment. You will get your home paid off faster. Do you ever find yourself in a social activity that you no longer enjoy? Make your regrets and spend the time on something you truly take pleasure in.

Forget the Past!

If you overspend on that pair of shoes or eat too much at a holiday party, don't beat yourself up, just start over again. You are better off to reach a three year goal in four years than never at all. Keep your nose pointed forward!

16

Especially for, But Not Limited to, Women

While past generations of women could often avoid making financial decisions, women today no longer can. What is different?

Several things! Women are living longer. Statistically women can expect to live to age 82. That means they will live longer in retirement than their mothers and grandmothers did, who by the way were largely able to rely on Social Security. Social Security alone does not translate to a comfortable lifestyle by today's standards. If a woman is married, she can expect to outlive her husband by 7 years. That means women need to know how to handle their finances as they will likely be in complete charge of them sometime in their lifetime.

Let's review some other statistics. Twenty percent of women never marry; forty-eight percent of first marriages and fifty percent of second marriages end in divorce; seventy-five percent of married women are eventually widowed.

The best time to start learning about investing is now. In our practices David and I often see the husband as the chief decision maker of investing, although many wives are the ones who do the day to day bill paying. We encourage the wives to take an interest in the overall estate and financial planning as we know through experience how overwhelming financial management can be when the responsibility is thrown on a person due to death of a spouse or divorce. We do find, as a trend, that husbands are agreeing with this philosophy but it still comes down to the wife wanting to take an interest in these matters.

For starters, if you are working, sign up to participate in your company's retirement plan and contribute the maximum each month. Do not assume that since your husband contributes to his, you don't need to have a retirement plan also.

Yes, yes you do! You both want the maximum savings automatically going from your paychecks into tax deferred retirement plans.

If you are not employed, but your spouse is, you may qualify for your own IRA, called a spousal IRA. For the year 2004 you may contribute $3,000 or if you are over 50 years old, your contribution can be a total of $3,500.

Finding Time

We know it takes time and fortitude to get started with investing if it is foreign to you. We can't do anything about the fortitude, you have to provide that, but check out the following survey results on how the average American spends time:

4 hours a week cooking
9 hours a week eating
5 hours a week reading
13 hours a week on family & pet care
18 hours a week watching TV/Internet

If you can squeeze an hour out of the above by reading newspaper and magazines and internet sites that focus on financial affairs, you will amaze yourself at the wealth of information you will accumulate. Smart Money magazine and Smartmoney.com are great places to start. Daily articles printed on Morningstar.com are helpful once you begin to understand the investment jargon. There are tons of books from basic to advanced investing just waiting for you at the library.

Finding Help

A number of years ago I attended night classes at a community college for a Personal Finance class just to see if it was worth recommending to some of my clients. It was! I continue to highly recommend these informative yet enjoyable classes. It's a great place to ask questions without feeling uncomfortable as everyone else in the class is there to learn too. You will feel empowered and more confident about yourself. And if you have a really good instructor, you can have fun while learning.

How about those Ladies' Investment Clubs? I did join one earlier in my career and have mixed reviews which I will share. Their popularity has lessened, perhaps due to the three bear markets which instilled frustration with steadily sinking stock prices and subsequent losses by members. There have been by many accounts by friends of mine who have been members of different clubs of anguished debate, disappointing returns, and having to use the exhaustive and often infuriating Stock Selection Guide (the official guide from the National Association of Investment Clubs) as a tool for analyzing securities. In our club we often spent more time on its permutations than the discussions of stocks. All that being said, it was a great learning experience. We had a wonderful bunch of ladies and shared many laughs while attempting to conquer the stock market. Again, these can be a supportive environment to gain knowledge.

Next step, find a financial advisor. That person should be a professional whose business is investing and someone with whom you can bond. You need to feel confident and comfortable with this advisor or your efforts will be wasted. For example, I have heard a number of women say they were embarrassed to ask questions of their old advisors or that they felt they were being talked down to. That relationship will get you nowhere.

Ask friends for referrals or contact the Financial Planning Association at FPA.com, which can lead you to lists of planners in your area and their special-ties. Don't feel shy about requesting an interview with potential counselors. A competent planner will want that interview to make sure you are a good fit for his/her company also.

One of the surest ways to lose money is to sit on it. Why? Because long term security is most threatened by inflation. The only real protection is growth, which will increase the size of your portfolio.

Regardless of your going it alone or with financial planner, there are four basic investment rules:

Start Now! Money must earn money, and the sooner your start the larger your pot will grow.

Stick With It! Investments grow best when regular infusions of new money are made. Don't try to time the market—that is like trying to use a crystal ball and it doesn't work. If it did, most stock brokers would be retired by the time they were 30. Buying when the market is down is smarter but harder! You will also want to buy when the market is up—it's easier as our human nature wants us to buy when everyone else is buying and we usually want to buy what everyone else is buying. Consistent investment and emotional discipline are important.

Diversify! You are more vulnerable to losing money if you have all your money in one place. Any investment can have a bad year, but usually when one type of investment is down, another will be up. A well diversified portfolio should have some buffer in it.

Be Open Minded! While your comfort zone might be having CDs at the bank, you risk limiting your earnings when interest rates are low as well as losing purchase power because of inflation. Expand your portfolio to include other choices, such as bonds, stocks and mutual funds to carry you through different market conditions.

The Unexpected

Coping with the unexpected can be traumatic to either spouse. The end of a marriage often means major financial changes for both. Since half of marriages end in divorce, there is good basis for concern. Knowing the assets and the debts of the marriage are important for both parties. There are certain things you can do to mitigate potential financial problems during a divorce. Obtain a credit card in your own name; establish your own checking and savings accounts; cancel all joint lines of credit, home equity lines, and freeze joint brokerage accounts. Even if you have an amicable divorce, these moves are things that will have to be done eventually anyway. Review all life insurance policies, annuities, retirement plans, wills and trusts to change beneficiaries if appropriate.

Be cautious about your divorce settlement as there are more important things than just getting it over with. Chief among them is considering the long term implications of dividing assets. One issue is taxes. If you own investment real estate, for example, you owe no taxes when you divide it but if you later sell it, you may have capital gains taxes and state taxes due on it. Another consideration is the diversity and quality of investments that you might receive. You don't want a portfolio concentrated in only one or two stocks or one that you can't liquidate unless you understand implicitly what you are getting.

If you were married ten years or longer before your divorce, you are entitled to receive Social Security based on your ex-husband's earnings, even if he has remarried. This does not take anything away from him as this is between you and the Social Security office. His benefits are not diminished but it can be important if your own benefit would be less or you wouldn't quality for Social Security on your own.

Gender matters. While this chapter is not meant exclusively for women, it is a fact that there are five times as many widows as widowers. As a woman, you must be prepared to make financial decisions. They may be sweeping changes or small ones designed to stretch limited dollars as far as they will go. Pension plans, where a couple receive a monthly check after retirement, can be paid out as joint and survivorship annuity, meaning after one death the payment continues on as is until the second spouse's death. However, pensions can also be paid out as a single life annuity, meaning no more checks after the death of the first spouse or perhaps a check but at a reduced amount. You both need to know the terms of the pension plan. If you are named as the beneficiary on your spouse's IRA, 401-k, or other retirement plan, the money is paid to you directly after the death. You may roll-over these funds into your own IRA without owing any taxes until you begin to withdraw the money. If you do not rollover the funds, you will have to pay the federal and state income taxes just as if you were receiving a paycheck for that amount of money.

If you are due to receive insurance policy benefits, you will not be taxed on that money as the beneficiary. However, the amount of the money you receive will be considered a part of your spouse's estate and can be taxed for federal estate tax purposes. This is another reason that estate planning through a Revocable Living Trust should be done.

Adventures!

A common remark that we hear from singles is that they would like to travel but haven't got anyone to go with. Many retiree group tours, and we hesitate to even use that term because it connotes a sedentary vision, are in reality educational, cultural, and athletic adventures that can enrich and inspire your life, not to mention adding some spice to it! These tour groups can provide opportunities to see new places and make new acquaintances. Your travel arrangements can be easier and more economical than doing it solo! Check these out to give yourself some food for thought! Biking, golfing, rafting, hiking, snowmobiling, historical tours, wine country tours, cooking class tours in France and Italy, cruises, educational tours, volunteer tours, and so much more. It is a big world out there!

Senior World Tours (888) 355-1686 or www.seniorworldtours.com
Over the Hill Gang International (719)389-0022 or www.othgi.com
Elderhostel (877) 426-8056 or www.elderhostel.org

17

An Awesome, Incredible, Important Investment Move!

Systematic investing—doesn't sound exciting or sexy but it truly is one of your greatest tools for wealth accumulation. It involves two time-honored tenets—systematic saving and sound risk management—in an investment strategy called dollar cost averaging.

Let's look at the mechanics of this dollar cost averaging. It is simply the process of investing in a fixed dollar amount in a stock or mutual fund at regular intervals. For example, you want to save $2,000 each quarter. In doing so, you will purchase more stock or mutual fund shares in the months when the price is low and fewer when the price is high. The ultimate result? A lower average cost per unit over time.

Here is a simple illustration of how this works: You put the $2,000 into a mutual fund every quarter. At the end of March, you buy 125 shares at a value of $16 per share. Your next purchase is at the end of June, when the share price has gone up to $20. By the close of September, your $2,000 buys approximately 87 shares at $23. Finally, at the end of the year prices are down to $21 as share and you buy approximately 95.

So how did you do? Your $8,000 investment bought 407 shares at an average cost of $19.65 per share. What would have happened had you simply decided to buy 100 shares every three months instead of spending a fixed dollar amount? Your outlay would be the same $8,000 however your average cost per share would have been $20 instead of $19.65.

That is the first benefit of Dollar Cost Averaging, a way to save on the ultimate cost of shares. Although the strategy doesn't insure that you'll sell high, it at least follows the other half of the maxim—buy low—by forcing the purchase of additional units when the prices are down.

Making It Easy for Yourself!

Another benefit is that when the strategy is set up, you pay yourself first and you can't cheat yourself by spending the money! It goes directly from your paycheck or checking account into your investment account. It is about as painless a way to save as you can get.

Next, and so importantly, it forces you to invest at the same frequency in good markets as well the bad. And decisions about how much to invest, when to invest and at what price to invest—which can all lead to procrastination—are eliminated.

Lessening Risk

Another factor which makes this such an incredible process is that Dollar Cost Averaging may help you to control risk. The fact that you are purchasing shares over a wide range of prices effectively cushions the impact of extreme market fluctuations on your investment's performance. Consequently, Dollar Cost Averaging may be particularly appropriate for individuals investing in sectors that are subject to an unusual degree of volatility, such as technology or emerging markets.

While it's tempting to think you can get into the market before a surge and bail out before a crash, this practice, known as market timing, is something that even the financial pros can't do well on a consistent basis. Why? Basically because much of the market's gain occurs on just a few days, missing any of them can have a big impact on returns.

According to a University of Michigan study that examined the stock market from 1963 to 1993, individuals who were invested in the market during this entire period would have average an annual return of 11.83%. However, those who were out of the market on the 30 days is gained the most would have earned an average annual return of just 8%. And those who missed the 90 best days would have reaped a mere 3.2%.

How to put Dollar Cost Averaging into Practice:

Payroll Deduction Plans
There are several easy ways to make Dollar Cost Averaging work for you. If you're participating in a company sponsored retirement plan, such as a 401-k, which features payroll-deducted contributions, you're already following this strategy. Some employers even offer workers the opportunity to fund their IRA's through payroll deductions. In all of these cases, the primary ingredients of dollar cost averaging—consistent contributions made on a regular schedule—are firmly in place.

Systematic Investment Programs
Another option is to establish a systematic investment program through a financial institution like a mutual fund company or a brokerage. You simply specify how much money you want transferred from your bank or checking account and how often, and the funds are automatically withdrawn and invested according to your instructions.

Stock and Mutual Fund Dividend Reinvestment Plans
Stock dividend reinvestment programs are still another possibility. These plans, which are available only through certain companies, allow stockholders to use their dividends to directly purchase additional company shares. Although these programs, popularly known as DRIPS, do not follow dollar cost averaging in the strictest sense (i.e., as the number of shares grows, so does the dollar amount to be invested), their fixed investment schedule and the opportunity to accumulate more shares over time make them a sound way to save. Of course, the same can be said of the dividend reinvestment programs available through most mutual fund companies.

David Bach, author of the best seller "The Automatic Millionaire" is a strong proponent of forgetting about budgets, forgetting about the get rich quick schemes and to just pay yourself first and make that payment an automatic thing. We totally concur with him.

18

The Bathtub Approach to Investing!

Picture you and your spouse sitting in your bathtub. You will be concentrating on three things, the level of the water you are sitting in; the faucet where you control the water flowing into the tub; and the drain where the water will flow out.

That in essence is financial planning—we keep the income or water flow into the bath at a level that is sufficient to keep you comfortable and we monitor these levels so not too much goes down the drain via spending. We also monitor the water temperature to keep it comfortable, not too hot, with high risk investments that are not appropriate for your particular risk tolerance, and not too cold with all low risk investments that won't let you keep abreast of inflation.

This chapter is devoted to how you can accomplish this endeavor and so let's start with the basics.

BONDS

Bonds are debt investments, meaning you loan a company your money and it pays you back that money plus interest. The advantages of bonds are that you can obtain regular income from the interest payments and your return of principal is usually considered safe if you hold the bond to its maturity date, the date when the loan is due. Bonds also have low correlation to the stock market, which means in an oversimplified statement, that bonds are usually up when the stock market is down. This low correlation does allow us to introduce less volatility in a portfolio over the long haul. Bonds, like all investments, do have risks, such as if you invest when interest rates are low you could be locked in to income that is not keeping up with inflation for the bond term. In these cases your principal could suffer a loss of value also if you have to sell the bond prior to the maturity date as buyers are less likely to want a bond currently paying 3% interest when new bond issues for sale are paying 4.5%. Some bonds can be redeemed, or paid off, prior to the maturity date and then you are stuck trying to find another place to reinvest the money. If that happens in a down market and you are counting on a certain income for living expenses, that could be a problem for your cash flow.

You can buy most bonds either as an individual issue, meaning a separate bond, or you can buy them in a bond mutual fund. In our office we normally do not buy individual issues for a client unless we can do so for a minimum of $100,000. The reasons are that there are transaction costs, or trading costs, which are not economical for smaller investment amounts and that you cannot get much diversification if you are working with less than $100,000. For individual issues we normally ladder them, in other words we buy varying maturity dates, say 2006, 2008, 2010, to get a variety of interest rates and lessen the client's market timing risk.

But don't be discouraged if you don't have a $100,000 minimum to buy the bonds. With an investment of $500 initially (less if you are going to do an automatic purchase every month) you can buy bond mutual funds. That means you put your money along with lots of other investors' money and the bond fund manager goes out and buys a variety of types of bonds with differing maturity dates. There are several advantages to bond mutual funds, such as immediate liquidity should you need to sell your shares, and there is more flexibility in price. As bond fund managers are constantly buying and selling bonds in the fund, you may stand a better chance of staying up with inflation by the continuous ingestion of new bonds being put in the fund pool. A bond fund can offer regular income, or you can elect to reinvest the income which will buy you more shares of the fund. Bond funds do have the same risks of individual issues—that is there is the likelihood of principal repayment but it is not guaranteed, and earnings are vulnerable to inflation and interest rate changes.

There is a wide variety of types of bonds and investors will use the different kinds to accomplish various goals.

Corporate Bonds

These bonds are sold by profit seeking companies as a way of raising money for a range of activities, such as building new facilities or expanding operations. Companies may prefer to borrow as opposed to issuing additional shares of stock, which dilutes the value of the stock already in the market. Corporate bonds generally pay higher interest than other types of bonds, but they can be considered riskier. There are companies such as Moody's, that establish an A, B, C rating for the issue, giving investors an idea of the risk of that particular bond. You will pay ordinary income taxes on the interest generated by corporate bonds.

U.S. Treasury Bonds

The government sells U.S. Treasury bills, notes and bonds to raise money to finance the running of the government. There are also the series EE bonds which became very popular during World War II. U.S. bonds, being backed by the federal government, are about as principal risk free as one can get but that comes at a cost as the interest rate paid is lower than what you could get with other types of bonds. You will owe federal income taxes on the interest you earn, but not state or local taxes.

Agency Bonds

These bonds are issued by various government agencies, both in Washington, D.C., and around the country. Some of the more recognizable are those that provide home mortgage money, are the GNMAs and FannieMaes. The interest you earn on these is taxable so the rates are slightly higher than on other government bonds.

Municipal Bonds

These bonds raise money to pay for projects, such as new roads or schools, and sometimes the actual operation of the government agency who is selling them. These can be a very effective way to invest if you are in a high income tax bracket as there is no federal tax due on the interest and generally no state or local taxes issued in the municipality where you live. For example, if you live in Arizona and buy Arizona state bonds, you owe no taxes on the interest. However, if you live in Arizona and buy a California state bond, you will owe taxes in Arizona on the interest.

Inflation Guard Bonds

There is a new generation of bonds entering the bond world, those that guard against inflation. In other words, there is a mechanism for the stated interest rate to rise if certain inflation rates are reached. The better known are TIPS, the U.S. Treasury notes, and a wide variety of Senior Floating Rate Notes, which are bank notes that adjust their interest rates every 30, 60 or 90 days as inflation rises. The catch here is that because of this advantage, the basic offered interest rate is low.

Regardless of the type of bond you purchase, there are several things you will want to know about. The length of the bond is important. Generally speaking, the longer the term the greater risk. For example, a 20 year bond might be paying an interest rate that is acceptable to you now, but might be way below the rate of inflation in 12 years. We like to keep bond terms to less than 10 years in most cases. The call date of a bond means the issuer can redeem it earlier than the stated maturity date. For many people this is not an issue, but if you are on a slim fixed income, having the bond pay off early may impede your necessary cash flow. Not all bonds are "callable." You will want to check out the bond's rating to evaluate the balance between risk and reward. One of the better known rating services is Moody's. While the Series EE savings bonds are not as popular as they once were, there are literally millions of dollars worth of them in circulation that no longer pay interest. People tend to hold them in safety deposit boxes at the bank or in shoeboxes in the house. Do yourself a favor and see if interest is still being paid on your bonds. Your bank should be able to tell you or you can go on line to find out. If interest is no longer being paid, cash them in! You need to make your money work for you! One last word on the subject of bonds, we wholeheartedly recommend using the many different kinds to diversify investment portfolios.

Stocks, the Darlings of the Investment World:

Stocks are also called equity investments, as they are ownership shares in a business. When you buy shares, you actually buy part of the company. If it prospers you make money either because you're paid a share of the profits (dividends) or because the value of the stock increases, or maybe both. You can own stocks for as long as you want, buy or sell them as you wish. Some of the advantages of stocks are that they may increase in value over time and that growth is usually faster than the rate of inflation. Stocks may pay dividends, generating cash income. Historically, stocks have provided the best return on investment over the past forty years. Stocks have risks associated with them, such as volatility, or sharp change in value, especially in the short term. Performance of a stock is often a matter of investor perceptions and not necessarily based on fundamentals. For example, if investors anticipate high energy prices or rising interest rates, even though these things have not occurred, the stock market may decline. Investment in boom periods can mean paying high prices for shares but remember, we can only know if it was a boom period when we can look back at it. Many investors will pass on purchasing stock citing the shares are too expensive only to have them rise substantially later on. Conversely, investors may hold stock, thinking prices will rise thereby increasing their profit, only to find their stock value decreasing in cost. Ah, this is the challenge and excitement of being in the stock market! While we buy bonds to create income, stabilize a portfolio and preserve wealth, we consider stocks primarily as vehicles for growth that we eventually sell to make a profit.

To buy stock, you will pay a commission or a transaction charge. You will do the same when you wish to sell the stock, but in the interim holding the stock does not cost you anything. If you receive a dividend in that holding period you will have to pay taxes on it but otherwise no taxes will be due until you sell and then the taxes are due just on the profit (you hopefully made!). We caution people that buying small amount of stock is not cost effective as the transaction charges will quickly negate your return. We feel it best to have at least $3,000 to spend on the stock before making a purchase. If you are in the beginning of getting an investment portfolio started, buying mutual funds makes more sense economically plus you get immediate diversification. We'll discuss mutual funds in detail later in this chapter.

If you are out there buying stocks, you have many decisions to make! Do you want to buy stock of large companies with long histories such as General Electric? These companies, also known as blue chips, are considered the most stable but also carry the highest prices per share. They are more likely to pay dividends. These large cap companies generally have a capitalization of over $5 billion.

A little higher risk category is the mid cap or mid sized stocks. They usually will not pay dividends as they use their cash for business expansion, they may have greater growth potential and generally are lower priced than the larger companies. Their market capitalization is $750,000 to $5 billion.

Small caps, sometimes also referred to as emerging growth companies are the mavericks of the market. With capitalization of $750,000 or less, these start-ups present the most risk. They conceivably carry the greatest chance for profit.

We are often asked "I want to buy stocks. How do I start?" Maybe spending a little time reading before leaping will save you future hand wringing. Read shareholder letters as that is going right to the source to see what the company's current philosophy is. Read the annual reports. Yes, they are thick but they are loaded with important data. Read about behavioral finance. We investors do strange things when it comes to rationally buying stocks and even more so when it comes time to sell stocks. Understanding some of "what makes us tick" can help us overcome these emotions to act in a logical way.

When you are considering buying a particular stock, there are several questions you will want to find answers for. Are the company's earnings growing? What is the P/E ratio? The P/E ratio is one standard of measure of a stock's worth and is computed by dividing the current price per share by the company's earnings per share. P/Es can range from 1 to 166+. A P/E goes up when investors are willing to pay more for a stock because they believe they will make money. There is no right or wrong number for a P/E, although you might see 20 or so as a frequent number. Does the company pay dividends if cash flow is an important issue for you? What is going on in the economy at large that might affect the stock? Research is at your fingertips now with the internet. See Morningstar.com or SmartMoney.com or YahooFinance.com for starters.

Now you have purchased stock. Are you going to adopt a strategy of buy and hold, or are you going to actively trade? Remember for active trading, you will incur transaction charges that will eat into your profit.

Deciding when to sell is often more difficult than when to buy as we can become emotionally attached to our choices. Some investors go by the numbers—they sell when the stock has hit a certain low, as a way to limit their losses, or they sell when a stock has hit a certain high, reaping their profits. Another reason to sell is that a stock or at least a portion of it, regardless of how good it is, is that it dominates your portfolio. Too much concentration is risky. You want diversification as a great stock today may not be so great in six months. If something fundamentally is going wrong with the company, such as new competition stealing sales, you might want to unload. While you want to consider tax implications, such as taking a loss to offset other gains, we don't normally sell a good stock for that sole purpose.

Some of you will be pulling your hair about now. There are easier ways to invest and let's talk about one of them:

Mutual Funds

Mutual funds rely on fund manager expertise and investor money. You and others buy shares in a mutual fund and the collective assets are invested by a fund manager who decides what and when to buy and sell. This expertise is one of the advantages of funds as well as the fund will normally have from 20 to 100 companies' stock so you are immediately diversified. Another benefit is that you don't need to have thousands of dollars to start investing. Some will open an account for you with no cash as long as you agree to automatically invest a certain sum each month, perhaps as low as $25. As we have said before, this automatic savings is a great way to go and grow! As you invest, you will be buying more shares of the fund. The fund, if it is doing well, will earn interest and capital gains. These profits are passed to you as distributions and you can either take them for income or reinvest to buy more shares. There are over 9,500 mutual funds from which to choose, and these can be divided into three major categories.

Stock or equity funds buy shares of publicly traded corporations, and these funds can be further categorized by their specialty of buying for growth or value, buying only companies of a certain size, such as large cap, or buying only special sectors such as energy or technology.

Bond or income funds invest to produce current income. Some funds will buy only government securities, others only Munis, and others corporate bonds. Some funds will buy stock of companies that generate dividends. If you see Balanced Fund, that connotes a fund holding both stock and bonds.

Index Funds

Index funds are gaining popularity with investors. The performance of stock and bond investments is measured by a number of different indexes. Each index measures the current average performance—whether it is up, down, or flat—of a certain investment category against a benchmark, determined by its past performance.

The point of an index fund is to produce the same results as the index tracks. Its strategy is to buy and hold all the stocks or bonds included in that index. The goal of the index fund is to do the same as a particular part of the market.

The most popular are the Standard and Poor's 500 Index, Spiders, the Dow Index, and Diamonds. Because index funds have little turnover, they only change when one company comes off the index and is replaced by another, they have lower transaction or trading costs. And because they are more passively managed, the fund expenses in general are lower than a typical mutual fund.

Let's discuss the cost of buying mutual funds. You will hear the term loaded funds or no-loads. The first term simply means there will be a commission paid to whoever sells you the fund. It can be a front-end load, usually called a Class A Share, which is the most common and generally that figure is around 5% if you are investing less than about $25,000. That commission will decrease as your investment increases, through a process called breakpoints. Be sure to ask whoever you are dealing with what the breakpoint numbers are as you can save by making smart purchases. There are back-end loads, known as Class B Shares, which charge you a commission if you sell your shares within a certain period of time, often five or six years. Personally, I do not encourage anyone to buy Class B Shares. It may seem that you are saving money as there is no front end commission but the mutual fund company assesses a higher expense ratio to Bs than if you buy As. There is no free lunch! Another type of share, called a Class C, often charges 1% annually for a number of years and may convert to a Class A after six or seven years. We consider these an acceptable way to go.

For no-loads, while a commission is not charged by the fund company, your investment advisor will charge an annual management fee and this is very popular. It is also a very simple way to be charged and to understand exactly what you are charged!

The funds prospectus explains its fees, expenses and whether or not there are sales charges. You will always want to read the prospectus before investing in any fund as it includes all the vital data you need to make a knowledgeable decision.

An investor is normally best rewarded with mutual funds if he is looking for steady progress, and not quick turnovers for profit. Again, the internet makes judging a fund's returns against its peers or against the market relatively easy.

Yield and Return

When investing, you will want to understand that YIELD is INCOME you receive as a percent of what your investment cost you; RETURN is the total of INCOME PLUS CAPITAL GAINS as a percentage of what your investment costs you.

You can begin to invest with confidence by following several basic principles:

You measure your investment reward by return or yield.

You manage risk, or the chance of getting poor or no returns, by making a variety of investments, such as stocks and bonds.

Allocation is figuring out what percentage of your portfolio goes into bonds, stocks, cash, real estate, etc.

Risk

Let's talk about risk because if you want the rewards of successful investing, you will be having to take some risks. How much and what kind are subjects of your comfort level. The higher risk category would include investing in products you don't understand, investing in products that sound too good to be true, such as that "guaranteed 25% return," focusing on quick profits, investing money you cannot afford to lose in riskier ventures, and investing in one single project.

More moderate risk includes taking more risk with a small part of your portfolio, expanding your portfolio into new or different areas, buying the largest portion of your portfolio into equities.

A lower risk strategy is investing in a balanced portfolio, selecting investments suited to meeting specific goals, being patient with long term growth, buying well established mutual funds, stocks or bonds, keeping an emergency cash fund equal to three or six months worth of living expenses.

What kind of risks will you be subjected to? Market risk is best known and it is what can happen if the stock market declines and you have to sell your investments at that particular time. If you can wait until prices rebound, you might avoid a loss. Interest rate risk has several perils. When interest goes up, inflation increases. The price of bonds declines since the current bonds will be paying less than newly issued bonds. The money you are earning on those bonds will buy less. Plus, higher rates may also mean that stock prices decline as investors move money out of stocks into more interest paying investments. If you have investments in international issues, they will be subject to valuation ups and downs to correspond with foreign currency fluctuations. Time invested risk, or volatility poses a big investment risk in the short term. Volatility is the speed with which an investment gains or loses value. Over the past 75 years, each major drop in the stock market has been followed by long term recovery. If you look at the big picture, you will discover that what appears to be a huge drop in prices in the market evens out when it's part of a longer term pattern.

Those are the technical aspects of risk, but let's look at how that personally affects us. You probably think you are a better driver than your spouse—we all do! Your grandkids are the brightest and the cutest! You are a confident investor who can handle the stock market world.

People routinely overestimate their ability to handle situations and this trait can be costly when it comes to your investment portfolio. There is more to dealing with portfolio risk than what is in your portfolio and we'll start off with your job. The stability of your income is very important regarding the risk you take with your investments. People in professions that are subject to economic changes such as real estate and construction could be in trouble if they lose their job while the market is down. If you need to sell stocks to generate income you will most likely incur losses. This scenario is less likely to befall a bank employee.

You know intellectually that the market will have its ups and downs, but how much down can your tummy handle? Think in dollar terms not percentages as the dollars have more impact. You may think you can stand a loss of $50,000 but if after seeing your portfolio decrease by $30,000 you can no longer sleep, you may need to move to a less risky portfolio allocation.

Lastly there is the issue of your time horizon. If you aren't going to retire for 10 years but need to make up for lost time in savings, you might think you want riskier investments that could return a better investment. However, if you are hand wringing at every market dip, you might need to work towards your goals by another approach, that is saving more, even at a hardship for your current living style, and invest in more stable type products.

Moderation

Moderation in all things is supposed to be good for us and that is certainly true in investing when we study diversifying our portfolios. You won't automatically diversify yourself by buying sheer numbers of different funds randomly. You want to plan your diversity with thoughts to the present and the future. In other words, if you are fortunate to get a healthy pension from your employer when you retire, you may not want as many income producing investments as someone who has no pension. If you are in your 30's you will probably want more growth type investments than someone who is in their 70's. If one of your goals is to pay a child's college tuition in a year or two, you will want to protect principal more than if the child starts college in 15 years. The challenge in obtaining a balanced and diverse portfolio is having investments that produce growth, provide income, preserve principal, contains investments that do well in an up market and some that do well when the market is down, having investments that outstrip inflation, and ones that invest internationally as well as domestically.

So how does one allocate his portfolio to accomplish his goals and manage his risk tolerance? Let's start with the basic premise of allocation. Cash provides the lowest returns generally; bonds produce the best returns in some years; stocks provide the highest and most consistent returns over the long term; no one sector has the best returns every single year.

Okay, this tells us you need a minimum of the three asset classes mentioned above. You can start out simply—20% cash and 30% bonds and 50% stocks. If you aren't able to invest in all three immediately, usually a balanced mutual fund, one combining stocks and bonds, is the place to start. If you need or want to change it to a more or less risky portfolio, you can do it. The main thing is to keep investing.

REITS

Once you have your core holdings in good order, there are plenty of other asset classes you can add to further round out your portfolio, such as real estate, energy, emerging growth and so on. We will give REITs special mention here as they are an investment with low correlation to the stock market. An over-simplification is that when real estate is up, the stock market is down and vice-versa. We like to add REITs to clients' portfolios primarily for this non-correlation.

Most REITs are mutual funds that invest in real estate. It could be a fund that invests in a variety of real estate throughout the nation or one that specializes in huge retail malls or large apartment complexes. The goal of the REIT is to produce income, usually on a monthly basis for the investors. While there is no guarantee, you might guard against loss by only investing money you won't need to redeem at a particular time, say when the real estate market might be down. Real estate has its cycles just as the stock market does.

Hedge Funds

Another option after your core holdings are secured might be a hedge fund. Hedge funds aim for absolute positive returns, and are not directly tied to the performance of any market. Years ago hedge funds were available only the wealthy or institutional investors who had at least a million dollars to invest. Today, they are still often limited to the sophisticated and accredited investor, meaning you are worth at least one million dollars and/or earn at least $200,000.00 in annual income. But if appropriate for you, you can gain access with a $50,000 minimum investment in many cases now. These are considered risky, as noted by the requirement that one be an accredited investor, because the managers are not limited or regulated like typical mutual funds. There are usually no uniform measures of performance, risk or disclosure. Notwithstanding all that, they are becoming a vehicle of investment choice for many people.

Other Alternative Investments

For those continuing to search for investments that do not correlate to the stock market, there are Managed Futures, Oil and Gas Investments, Equipment Leasing and Tax Lien Certificates and Tax Credits. All these alternative investments carry a greater degree of risk but also add greater diversification for the appropriate investor.

Annuities

Another vehicle for investment is the tax deferred annuity, which can be either a fixed rate or a variable rate instrument, issued by an insurance company. A fixed annuity allows an investor to contribute funds that accumulate tax deferred for a specific rate of return, similar to a certificate of deposit at a financial institution. Variable annuities are a different animal. They are a wrapper enclosing sub-account mutual funds whose growth is tax deferred until distributions are taken. They have a tendency to get some bad press because they are often used inappropriately. Personally only about 25% of our clients have them and it is always for a specific use. A good annuity contract will have a minimum death benefit. For example, an investor puts $100,000 into the annuity which invests in sub-account mutual funds. Three years later the market is down, and the annuity is valued at only $65,000. The annuity owner dies but the beneficiaries will collect the original $100,000 (sometimes with interest on top of that) regardless of its drop in value in a down market. Conversely, if the market value at time of death is $150,000, the beneficiaries will collect that amount. In other words, the annuity beneficiaries will have no loss of principal and stand to participate in the up-side potential of the stock market. But there is no free lunch, and annuities have surrender charges if the owner decides to liquidate before the maturity, often a seven year period. Also, these annuities have considerable expenses involved that decrease net return to the annuity owner, particularly in the early years of the contract. One never wants to invest in a variable annuity unless they are using money that will not be needed during that surrender period. Different contracts will have different terms and conditions and you want to understand the fine print before jumping into this investment. Always read your prospectus before investing.

What Should I Do?

We've discussed the investment choices. What should you do first?

Without question, maximize your tax deferred retirement plans. If you are an employee, your choices should be easy. They are whatever your company offers such as a 401-k plan, a 457, or a 403b plan. Your maximum contribution for 2004 is $13,000 unless you are age 50 or older, then you can sock away $16,000. After you have filled that up, do a spousal IRA if you have a non-working spouse. The maximum contribution for him or her is $3,000 unless age 50 or older, then it is $3,500 annually. A limitation is that if you earn $160,000 Adjusted Gross Income, the contribution will not be deductible.

If your employer does not have a retirement plan, your options will be either a traditional IRA or a Roth IRA.

The Traditional IRA:

Who can contribute?
Anyone with earned income before the tax year in which the age 70 ½ is attained.

Key Features:
Contributions are allowed regardless of the individual's Adjusted Gross Income. Contributions may be deductible. Tax deductibility depends on salary level and whether the IRA owner participates in an employer sponsored retirement plan. The maximum contribution is $3,000 unless if age 50 or older, then it is $3,500. Contributions must be made by April 15th to be considered a prior year contribution.

Roth IRA:

Who can contribute?
Contributions are not allowed if the individual's income exceeds the adjusted gross income of $110,000 for a single and $160,000 for joint tax filers.

Key Features:
Contributions are nondeductible but they accumulate tax free. Permits tax free and penalty free withdrawals on contributions at any time. Contributions allowed after turning age 70 ½. Contributions must be made by April 15th to be considered a prior year contribution.

If you are **self-employed**, you may choose either the IRA or the Roth IRA, however if you wish to contribute more to your retirement, there are a number of plans available to you. Several of them have minimal paperwork and reporting.

The Individual 401-k Plan (Our favorite!)

This plan is designed for the employer with no employees except a spouse. Contributions may be discretionary. Participant loans are available. All contributions must be 100% vested immediately. Combined contributions cannot exceed the lesser of the 100% of compensation or $40,000.00.

The Simplified Employee Pension (SEP) Plan

This plan works for self-employed person, partnerships, corporations and non-profits. It has minimal paperwork and reporting. Employers can change their annual contributions. Deductible employer contributions are made directly to employees IRA's and are 100% vested immediately. The 2003 annual contribution cannot exceed the lesser of 25% of an employee's eligible compensation or $40,000.

The Simple IRA

Designed for self-employed persons, partnerships, corporations, and non-profit entities with 100 or less employees. Employees may defer up to $8,000 (or $9,000 if age 50 or older). The employer must choose from one of two options: match employees contribution dollar for dollar, up to 3% of compensation, or contribute 2% of each eligible employee's compensation (maximum eligible compensation is $200,000).

Once you have maximized your contributions to your tax deferred retirement plans, you will want to save as much as you can for that retirement nest egg in regular savings. But to do that wisely you will need to set your financial goals, create a timetable and design a portfolio to best meet your objectives. We've talked about safe ways to go about it on your own if that is your only option right now, but ideally you will want to go through the formal financial planning process when you are able to do so.

So What Actually is a Financial Plan

It is a road map that will take you from point A, where you are today, through short-term goals, things you want to be able to afford within the next year or two; through mid-term goals for big ticket items further down the road, to the long-term goals of your retirement lifestyle and perhaps a legacy for your heirs.

A wise person once said, "Even the longest journey begins with a single step." Let me walk you through the process as if you were considering working with our firm as your financial advisor.

We meet for a free consultation, an opportunity for us mutually to explore whether we will be a good fit. At this meeting we want to get to know you—your current situation, the goals that you are hoping to accomplish, and what role you see a financial advisor playing in that process. You will want to know what services we provide, what the costs are and if you feel a comfortable relationship can be established.

If we proceed, we expect to provide you with help in defining your goals, explanations for investment opportunities and common mistakes, a structured, individualized strategy for investing, advice on specific investments, implementing the investment plan, monitoring how well your investments are doing towards meeting your goals, and help with understanding and managing risk. It is a continuing process that will be modified as your life's experiences change.

How do we do all this? We start off by compiling a financial plan. The first section of the plan is a snapshot of all your current assets, including real estate, stocks, bonds, mutual funds, retirement plans and so forth.

Next, we incorporate your life's goals, from immediate to long term and delineate the contributions that you will be making towards those goals. Lastly, we research every stock, bond and mutual fund that you currently own and will include our recommendation as to it being one you should hold, hold some of, or sell. We base our recommendations on a number of things—is the investment fundamentally sound, does this investment work with the other investments in your portfolio to effectively help you reach your goals, is there too much of one investment which could add unnecessary risk, are you well diversified per your risk tolerance, what are the tax implications of holding it or selling it, are there special issues such as restricted stock options which require special handling?

For those of you who might be interested further in the mechanics of our financial plans, we subscribe to Modern Portfolio Theory. Based on research by Nobel-prizewinning economists Harry Markowitz and William Sharpe, this view of investing says that by combining different asset classes, large cap stocks, small foreign stocks, bonds, real estate, energy and so forth, you can minimize risks and maximize your returns. Modern portfolio theory demonstrates the particular mix of assets that will give you the highest return for the level of risk you are willing to accept. We do not, by the way, accept a new client without first doing a financial plan as we feel strongly that we cannot do our best for that person without having such a road map to follow and continuously monitor. Part of that monitoring includes rebalancing. Rebalancing is a process that we generally do towards year end to bring the portfolio back to the original allocation, say 60% stocks and 40% bonds. If stocks experienced great growth during the year, the portfolio might now be 80% stocks and 20% bonds, so we sell 20% of the stocks and buy 20% more bonds. Rebalancing means going against the natural tendency to run from pain and toward pleasure as you can see we are selling stocks that did well to buy bonds that were lower. But remember the premise "Sell High and Buy Low". That is exactly what rebalancing forces one to do. It helps to capture gains prior to down cycles and discourages the urge to time the markets.

Where To Go For Professional Advice

Most financial services institutions, such as brokerages, banks, mutual funds and insurance companies provide investment advice and financial planning. They pay advisors who work with them either a salary or a commission on the investments they sell. Or they may be Fee Planners, such as ourselves, who charge an annual fee on the amount of assets they are managing for the client. Advisors should always be clear about what their services cost and how they are assessed. That will help you to evaluate the investment choices they offer and pick out what is best for you.

I admit I am prejudiced. I am a Certified Financial Planner™ Practitioner (CFP®) and while someone having this certification doesn't necessarily mean they are going to be right for you as your advisor, you will at least know they completed a rigorous study schedule, usually taking several years, had to qualify for the experience requirements, had to pass a 10 hour test that only about half pass the first time around. You can contact the FPA (Financial Planning Association) at (800) 322-4237 or www.fpanet.org to get a list of CFPs® in your area. The web gives information about their specific practices also and is a good research tool.

Another great place for referrals can be a CPA or an estate attorney. Banks, credit unions, insurance agents, and stockbrokers will provide varying degrees of investment advice and financial planning. Most of our business comes in from referrals from our clients so ask family, friends, colleagues who they are working with. Attending classes and seminars will familiarize you with different styles of advisors and advice.

What Should I Expect to Pay?

There are different services provided by different planners depending on their type of practice. In our office, we do not take on a new client without doing a formal financial plan as we previously stated. These plans will range in a one time fee of anywhere from $500 to $3,500+ depending on the complexity of the client's situation.

If the client then wishes us to manage their investment portfolio, we charge an annual fee based upon the assets under management. This is called "Fee Based" and charges are generally from ¾% to 2.5%, depending on the size of portfolio.

There are some situations where an investor may prefer an hourly charge, such as someone looking for a second opinion or researching an unusual circumstance. The hourly rates usually will range from $50 to $200 per hour. The going rates are often predicated upon where you are located, for example the cost of living is more in San Francisco than in Tampa Bay, Florida.

Most brokerage houses and insurance companies will charge you a commission on anything you purchase from them. You will find this quite common for investors who are just starting to invest or who have less than $100,000 in their portfolios.

Different people, different needs, different circumstances—it is your job to determine which planner and type of service is best for you. Never be shy about exploring what the planner will do for you and understanding exactly what the charge to you will be. If the person you are meeting with cannot be clear on these two issues, run out the door!

Planning Overview

Even when using professionals to guide you through your financial and estate planning, there are some basics that you should be aware of to potentially maximize your results. Your priorities and objectives will probably change over time as life does throw us some unexpected curves. Maybe those annual month long trips to Europe have lost some of their appeal; perhaps helping a grandchild get through college has now become important. A change in your priorities might require a portfolio change to best accommodate these different goals. Keep yourself focused and then make sure you share that with your advisor.

Your tax situation may change over time. While we don't advise letting the tax issue be solely responsible for choosing the buy/sells in your portfolio, it should be a factor. For example, Municipal bonds, which are not subject to federal or state taxes, are great when you are earning wages and in a high tax bracket. They become less advantageous when you retire and your income tax bracket drops. Paying off your home when you have a sizable mortgage and are collecting a paycheck may not be the best tax move, but once you have paid down the loan to where it is principal only, you have lost the tax incentive so zeroing it out might be a good move.

Conference Room Lock-Down

Don't become so attached to an investment that it clouds the "to sell or not to sell" question. Believe me, after years of investment counseling I can guarantee you that people often give little thought to buying a particular investment but agonize over the thought of selling it. Keep in mind some of the basics to get you through the dilemma.

Forget what you paid! So you paid $100 per share for a tech stock in 1999 but it is only worth $18 today. The relevant question is this: Would you buy that stock today at its $18 price? If not, it's probably time to unload it. The behavioral scientists confirm that people feel the loss of $100 more than the profit of $200!

Ignore day to day price swings, but if the price is going down due to fundamental changes in the company, it is probably time to sell. If the price is going up and up, perhaps it is time to capture some profit. Remember, we buy stock to make a profit but that adage often gets forgotten.

Consider how much of your portfolio this investment represents. Are you too heavily loaded in this asset class? Are you too heavily loaded in this one stock? Don't put yourself at unwarranted risk.

Don't look back! Once you have made the decision, even if it took your financial advisor locking you in the conference room until you agreed to the sale, move forward.

Squeezing More Income Out of Your Portfolio

Fear sometimes immobilizes us. Your fear of outliving your investments might be causing you to not enjoy your present circumstances. We have seen this particularly after the three year bear market where some people were shocked by the decrease in value of their portfolios. It may be possible to have the same account value in your portfolio but in different investments so that your income can be increased. How to do that?

First, you will want some stocks that are dividend paying stocks, in other words they pay cash (technically a share of company profits) to stockholders usually on an annual basis. There are mutual funds that specialize in buying stocks of dividend paying companies so that is an option also. You may have non-dividend paying stocks or mutual funds that need to be replaced.

Next we recommend some bond moves. Depending on the amount you have to invest, you can do one, or both, of the following:

Buy bond mutual funds and have the income generated sent to your bank account every quarter. You might benefit most by diversifying the types of bond funds, such as government backed funds for the perceived safety and then some highly rated corporate bond to increase your yield.

If you have at least $100,000, you could buy individual bonds and ladder them. By that we mean each bond will have a different maturity date, such as 2007, 2008, and 2009. Laddered bonds provide an opportunity for you to obtain varying yields and they generate less reinvestment risk for your portfolio. As the bonds mature, you continuously buy new ones which offer the current yield rates. The interest from these bonds can be sent automatically to your bank account also. The reason we suggest $100,000 as a minimum for individual bonds is that you have transaction charges for each buy and for smaller amounts of money it is not cost effective.

Lastly, purchase some non-correlating asset classes, such as Real Estate Investment Trusts, or better known as REITS. You can buy these as mutual funds or you can buy them as Private Placement Offerings. Either way, REITS are designed to kick off income, usually on a quarterly basis. We are told by several of the major REIT companies that they are designed to return around 7% annually but of course nothing is guaranteed. Some REITS have done much more than that in some years and lost money in other years. It is the power of diversification and non-correlation to the stock market that can add benefit to a portfolio needing to spin off cash to the investor. REITs are subject to special risks such as illiquidity and are not necessarily suitable for all investors.

Money IN—Money OUT!

Most of this book has been about putting money into your accounts but you need to pay attention to which are the most beneficial ways of taking it out.

You always want an emergency fund. Depending on your circumstances, that might be anywhere from three to six months worth of living expenses sitting in a bank or money market account that provides easy access, as in being able to write checks to get to it.

Generally, you want to use money from your regular accounts (money that you already paid taxes on) first before drawing from your deferred accounts such as IRAs or other retirement plans. One exception to this rule is that when you are 70 ½, you will be required by the IRS to take your Minimum Required Distribution. The tax man cometh, at least he is lying in wait to get your retirement funds taxes but you may be able to manipulate that somewhat. Before you reach 70 1/2, withdraw from your deferred accounts just enough to take you to, but not over, the 15% tax bracket. That way when you hit the required distribution age, you will have smaller amounts that have to come out.

If you are under 59 ½, avoid drawing from your retirement accounts as you will pay federal and state income taxes plus a 10% penalty. If you live in a state like California, that could leave you with maybe 50% of your money, a very steep price to pay. There are exceptions to that rule, including a well known one called the SEPP (Substantially Equal Periodic Payments). You take distributions from your IRA for a five year term or until you reach 59 ½. The IRS has three different calculation tables that you can choose from but once you make a choice and start the process, it cannot be changed.

The other exceptions are:
Death, Disability, Deductible Medical Expenses in excess of 7.5% of your AGI, Qualifying medical insurance premiums for the unemployed, Qualified higher education expenses, and Qualified first time homebuyer, up to a limit of $10,000.

Be sure, by the way, to take your Required Minimum Distribution when required, even if you don't need the money, or the IRS will assess you a penalty of 50%. This is huge so don't overlook it.

If you have company stock in your retirement account you have two choices when you retire. You can either roll it over into your IRA or you can take out the shares. If you do the latter, you will pay taxes on the cost basis of the shares at the time you take them out. If you hold those shares then for at least a year, you will pay capital gains taxes, which are lower than income taxes, on the profit.

If you roll the shares into your IRA, you will pay ordinary income taxes on the whole amount in the year of withdrawal.

To muddy it up even more, the cost basis is handled differently in each scenario for your heirs. We strongly urge people faced with this to consult their CPA or financial advisor as the different options could have major implications to your estate planning.

19

Happy Ever After!

We have endeavored to give you practical and creative ideas to help you reach your lifestyle goals. You work for forty or fifty years, saving as much as you can, and then you spend the rest of your life living some kind of retirement. Let's dwell on the "some kind of retirement".

We know from studies that over half of Americans don't like their jobs and can hardly wait to leave. They may stay at a particular company for years with the sole goal of retiring. But they retire and are at a loss for what to do with themselves. A lack of new purpose for living can be hazardous to your emotional and physical health and that of your spouse.

We have two types of emotions, negative and positive. Positive feelings attract us; negative emotions make us want to take flight or fight.

We naturally want to avoid pain or threats or the unknown. It's more comfortable to go down the path of what we are familiar with rather than strike out on new roads. If you let negative emotions direct your life, it is easy to be fearful, cranky and withdrawn. Without a clear vision of what you want to do as a retiree, you will only move away from what you don't want. Your present and future life could be clouded by worries rather than happy anticipation.

You can make your retirement a wonderful time. Think of what makes you feel excited, things you truly have an interest in but perhaps up to now didn't have the time to explore. Understanding what makes you feel passionate, and then creating an outlet for them will bring you pleasure. Pleasure is a very good thing!

Bring purpose to your life if you want to experience more fulfilment in your daily life. Helping others or making progress with some of your goals will give you a sense of meaning.

Understand your strengths and use them to contribute richness to your life and the lives of those close to you. Avoid negative people; they can drain you. Embrace positive attitudes and positive people to help you increase the joy and fun in your life. Let's face it, there are certain times that you have to work harder at life—when you are starting on a new career path, when jobs, kids, their school and sports activities have to be juggled, dealing with a divorce, or adjusting to your retirement lifestyle. Some situations just require more emotional energy than others, but you always have the choice of your attitude in dealing with them.

We can empower ourselves as individuals, but what about that spouse of ours? You've been following your financial plan, denying yourself pleasures you could have had along the way (a double mocha latte' at least once a week wouldn't have broken the bank but you didn't do it!) but you are now at retirement and your spouse doesn't have the same interests in retirement that you do.

This is not uncommon. David and I have counseled numerous couples and regardless of their age, many have opposing personalities when it comes to spending and saving. This difference can become more pronounced when in retirement. You gave up those double mocha lattes because it would allow you to have them once you retired. You gave up your choice of cars to drive a used minivan so someday you could get that yellow Corvette you have lusted for since you were in your twenties. You compromised with keeping the old sofa for years so one day you could redecorate the living room. Now you are retired and you have some financial security but old spending habits die hard for some individuals. You may be married to one of those. Even if you are single, you may be having a difficult time getting into a comfort zone about what you actually can do with your money. Many, many, times we have urged clients to go and enjoy! Go travel, go get new hobbies, go shopping, go out for dinner, go learn, go volunteer, go have adventures, go make your retirement what you want of it! A couple may find their differences exacerbated by being retired.

You can save yourselves from this agony with good communication, and start this communication well before you are ready to retire. In retirement each partner should have equal say on how to spend money. On the other hand, each partner deserves consideration from the other regarding their wishes. Money and love conflicts usually require some forms of compromise. While you each may not get exactly what you want, if you both value each others desires, you can have a fulfilling life.

While we have dwelled more on differences here, let us finish with the positives. We know so many couples who have wonderful lives, enriched by doing what they had planned for and saved for most of their working years. We think the important ingredients for that success is their communication and also the excitement and sense of accomplishment they have together as they complete their goals along the way. Some wise person said the fun is not all at the destination, but also in the journey to get there!

About the Authors

Penny Eisenstein received the CERTIFIED FINANCIAL PLANNER designation from the College of Financial Planning in Denver, Colorado in 1998. She has twenty years combined experience in the financial and commercial real estate industries. In 1993, she attained the CCIM (Certified Commercial Investment Member) designation and has served on the Board of Directors of the CCIM Association for several years. She also is a member of the Financial Planning Association. She has managed over $40,000,000.00 of clients' assets and has hosted or co-hosted financial planning radio talk shows for over seven years on KTAR, KYFI, FCEO, and KPOP. Penny has a private pilot's license. She and her husband, David, live in San Diego, California.

David Eisenstein is an attorney, licensed to practice in both the states of California and Arizona. He earned his undergraduate degree from the University of Arizona in 1973, graduating with highest distinction as a member in the scholastic honor societies of Phi Beta Kappa and Phi Kappa Phi. In 1976 he received his Juris Doctor "with distinction" from the University of Arizona College of Law. David has 28 years of experience as a practicing attorney, emphasizing estate planning as well as being a nationally known litigator in the field of direct sales law. He has appeared before the California and Arizona trial and appellate courts and was admitted to the Bar of the U.S. Supreme Court in 1984. He has been both a member and officer of numerous community and professional groups over the years. David has hosted estate and financial planning radio talk shows on KCEO and KPOP. For relaxation, David enjoys the challenges of golf.

Their contact information is www.kmne.com

Offices are located at:

16980 Via Tazon, #B-220
San Diego, Ca. 92127
Tel (858) 674-1270, Ext. 22
Fax (858) 674-0870

0-595-33213-7